DEBUNKING THE PAGAN ROOTS OF CHRISTMAS

KEVIN L. BETTON JR.

GREATER WORKS DISCIPLESHIP MINISTRIES

Copyright © 2025 by Kevin L. Betton Jr.

All rights reserved.

No part of this publication may be reproduced, distributed, or transmitted in any form or by any means, including photocopying, recording, or other electronic or mechanical methods, without the prior written permission of the publisher, except in the case of brief quotations embodied in critical reviews and certain other noncommercial uses permitted by copyright law.

Scripture quotations marked CSB are from the Christian Standard Bible®. Copyright © 2017 by Holman Bible Publishers. Used by permission. Christian Standard Bible® and CSB® are federally registered trademarks of Holman Bible Publishers.

Qur'an quotations are taken from *The Qur'an*, translated by M. A. S. Abdel Haleem (Oxford: Oxford University Press, 2004).

Published by Greater Works Discipleship Ministries

ISBN (Paperback): 979-8-218-87216-8

ISBN (Hardback): 979-8-9940049-0-6

Unless otherwise indicated, all emphasis within quotations is the author's.

Printed in the United States of America.

First Edition: December 2025

Dedication

I want to first thank my Lord and Savior Jesus Christ. Without Your advent, none of this would be possible. It is an undeserved honor and privilege to serve in Your Kingdom. Thank You for aligning my life in a way that made this book possible. I pray it finds its way into the hands of every believer and convicts hearts about celebrating this holy day that honors the incarnation. I also pray it confronts the lies spoken from the lips and fingertips of anyone who would dare accuse our Creator of being a copycat. Let this book embody Titus 1:9—encouraging with sound teaching and refuting those who contradict it.

To my beautiful wife, Celeste. You are God's greatest gift to me. Thank you for always seeing the best in me, confronting the worst in me, and understanding the intention of my heart even when my execution falls short. I can't imagine doing life without you. Unbreakable.

To my amazing children, Kyndal, Mikayla, and Judah. I pray this book creates a legacy that empowers you to disciple your own families one day. Nothing will ever be as fulfilling as being your dad.

Kyndal, watching you grow has been such a joy. We built our relationship our way—Jesus and sneakers.

Mikayla, I pray the love you've experienced from me as a father only enhances your love for our heavenly Father. I will ALWAYS be there for you, no matter what.

Judah, my only son. You are a gift to this world. I pray you exceed everything your grandfather and I have accomplished. Chart your own path in life.

To my wonderful parents: thank you for the way you raised me. Even as a grown man, it is unbelievably affirming to hear you both say you are proud of me. Dad, thank you for all the Sunday school lessons—they're paying off. I'll bet you never saw this coming. Mom, you are the strongest, most elegant, and classy woman I know.

To my in-loves. I could not have asked for a better set of bonus parents. I love you both so much. You have made me feel like your own son from the moment you met me. I honor you both.

To my best friend, hype man, and biggest supporter—whose voice still gets deeper when he preaches — Cedric Jones — yes, you got a shout-out. You deserve it. Love you, bro.

Romina Betton, Tanika Asiedu, Chepren ("Hey Miss") Carter, Siobhan Rainey, Kimberly Graham, Dr. Roderick Merritt, and Kimberly Arnold—you all are family. I don't just love doing ministry with you; I love doing LIFE with you. Words cannot express how much I appreciate your unwavering support. Dopest team ever—and we have so much fun.

To the leaders who nourished this gift in me, beginning with my Sunday school teachers, Bishop Calvin Hooper Sr. and Minister Reggie. To the pastors who have shepherded me and my family:

Bishop Rodney and Elder Karen Gilchrist—your support in this season means everything. Serving the Kingdom through Liberty Christian Center is a delight; doing it under your faithful leadership is a joy. We honor you.

Apostle David and Pastor Sharon Davis—thank you for loving the Bettons, supporting us, challenging us, and disciplining us when necessary (meaning me). Greater Life Church will always be home, and you will always be family.

Bobby and Barbara Butler—thank you for stewarding a young married couple and giving us room to grow.

Robert and Charlean Woodall—you loved me and prayed me through the toughest season of my life. I will always cherish my time at Bible Way Hibner- Memorial COGIC.

Bishop Troy Anthony Bronner—completing this book the day after your passing is bittersweet. No one has inspired me to be a student of the Word like you. You are the best preacher I've ever met—a walking homiletical blueprint. Yet it is the way you and the Elim Christian Fellowship passionately loved Mikayla and me that I will forever remember. Rest well, Sir.

Finally, to the Army of Urban Apologists who continue to contend for the faith—it is an honor to stand beside such a God-glorifying, Christ-centered, Spirit-filled, Word-based community. Bodega, I love each and every one of you. Till the day the Lord calls us home, we will ensure every believer knows what they believe, why they believe it, how to defend it, how to share it, and how to live it.

Contents

1. Introduction — 1
2. The True Meaning of Christmas: God With Us — 5
3. The Date of December 25: Biblical and Historical Roots — 29
4. Saturnalia & Sol Invictus
   They Not Like Us — 60
5. Unwrapping Yule
   Facts Over Folklore — 77
6. Counterfeit Christs
   Exposing the Myth of Pagan Copycats — 83
7. The Man Behind the Myth
   How Alexander Hislop Created a Pagan Christmas — 113
8. Unmasking Santa
   The Saint Behind the Suit — 124
9. The True Roots of the Christmas Tree
   Chopping Down the Lies — 135
10. Liberty, Not Legalism: Why Celebrating Christmas Isn't Sin
    And Why No One Can Call It Pagan — 145

Bibliography 151

About the author 163

1

INTRODUCTION

In the documentary *Religulous*, comedian and writer Bill Maher travels to a reconstructed first-century village in modern-day Nazareth, Israel, and interviews an actor portraying Jesus. With a smirk, Maher asks, "Does it ever bother you that the story of a man who was born of a virgin and resurrected—your bio—was something that was going around the Mediterranean for at least a thousand years?" He continues, "We've got Krishna, who was in India a thousand years before Christ—Krishna was a carpenter, born of a virgin, baptized in a river..."

The actor, clearly unprepared for such claims, stumbles for a response: "Are you saying that was written in history?" Maher answers quickly, "Absolutely." Then, leaning in, he adds, "There's the Persian god Mithras, six hundred years before Christ—born on December 25th, performed miracles, resurrected on the third day, called the lamb, the way, the truth, the life, the savior, the messiah." The actor shifts uneasily, finally replying, "All I know is that I go by the Word of God. That's what I believe."

Maher didn't stop there. Later in the film, he confronts other tourists, claiming that according to the *Egyptian Book of the Dead* (1280 BC), the god Horus—the son of Osiris—was born of a virgin, baptized in a river by Anup the baptizer, tempted alone in the desert, healed the sick and blind, cast out demons, walked on water, raised Asar (which Maher says translates to Lazarus) from the dead, had twelve disciples, was crucified, and after three days was resurrected, with two women announcing him as "the savior of humanity."

For many Christians, hearing claims like these creates the same uneasy feeling seen on the actor's face. What would you say if a family member, a co-worker, or even your own child watched that documentary and came to you with these questions? Too many believers respond the same way he did: "All I know is that I go by the Word of God. That's what I believe." Far too many Christians respond in similar fashion to the claims of Christmas being a plagiarized copy of older pagan virgin birth myths. The fact-based claims and objections of unbelievers are often met with faith-based answers that, while they are sincere, fail to engage the evidence.

Documentaries like *Religulous* are becoming increasingly common, their claims even bolder and more persuasive. As a result, countless people have concluded that Christmas is indeed a pagan holiday—copied from religions that predated Christianity.

But here's the problem: none of Maher's claims about Mithras or Horus are even remotely true. In the chapters ahead, we'll uncover where these stories really came from, why they sound convincing, and how the historical evidence actually affirms — not undermines — the truth of the Christmas story.

I am what many people call a "PK," a preacher's kid. My father and mother ensured I grew up in a home where we were constantly reminded that "Jesus was the reason for the season." Each year our home was decorated with Christmas lights. We hung stockings, baked Christmas cookies, and watched popular Christmas movies like "The Grinch," "Miracle on 34th Street," and "Home Alone." Most of all, I can't ever remember a year without a Christmas tree that eventually became filled with gifts. We were the typical family that participated in all the Christmas traditions and I enjoyed every minute of it.

It never occurred to me to question the validity of the virgin birth or to ask how we know Jesus was born on December 25th. I was well over 40 years old before I ever heard any serious challenges to the traditional Christmas story. That ignorance was bliss. I treasure the memories of my childhood; however, I cannot afford to take this same approach with my children, and neither can you. My wife Celeste and I have three amazing children, two daughters who are in college and a teenage son. We are a beautiful, blended family. Years ago we adopted the practice of spending time each Christmas morning reading through the passages in the gospels that detail the birth of Jesus and having prayer prior to opening gifts. We adopted this practice in order to ensure our family, especially our children, understood *why* we celebrated Christmas and took part in the various traditions surrounding the season.

Furthermore, with the increased use of social media platforms like YouTube, Facebook, Instagram, and TikTok being used to distribute false information that spreads like wildfire, we wanted to ensure that our family was grounded in the truth and would not be persuaded by lies. Social media content creators are often far more concerned with creating viral videos, than promoting truth, and will often create and/or share information like that contained in *Religulous*, without ever fact-checking their claims.

As I learned about accusations of Christmas having pagan origins and associations, I did the best I could to share that information with my wife and older children along with apologetic rebuttals. This book is written for everyone who has heard, or ever will hear of Christmas being a copy of a pagan myth. Together, we will examine the evidence of the true origin of the Christmas holiday as well as the traditions that accompany it. We will demonstrate with convincing evidence, that Christmas is the celebration of the incarnation of Jesus Christ and in the process, debunk every claim of pagan origin.

2

THE TRUE MEANING OF CHRISTMAS: GOD WITH US

The word *Christmas* comes from Old English, the form of English spoken many centuries ago. It derives from *Christes mæsse*, literally "the Mass of Christ"—a church service held in honor of Jesus Christ. From its very inception, Christmas has always been about the incarnation, not the calendar. And that fact alone dismantles one of the most common internet claims — that Christmas was created as a date-first, theology-second holiday. History shows the exact opposite: Christians celebrated the event long before anyone cared about the calendar. This chapter explores the true meaning of that celebration—showing that Christmas was never meant to center on a date, but on an event: the moment when God became flesh. We'll build a biblical foundation here before turning in the next chapter to the history of *when* Christians chose to celebrate it.

From the very beginning, Christmas has been about the incarnation. The word *incarnation* literally means "enfleshment" or "embodiment in flesh."[1] Though the word itself doesn't appear in Scripture,

---

1. James D. G. Dunn, "Incarnation," in *The Anchor Yale Bible Dictionary*, ed. David Noel Freedman (New York: Doubleday, 1992), 397.

the concept clearly does—it describes the moment when the eternal Son of God took on human nature in the person of Jesus Christ.

The title *Christ* isn't a last name but a designation meaning "Anointed One." It comes from the Greek *Christos*, translating the Hebrew *māšîaḥ* (*Messiah*), derived from *māšaḥ*—"to anoint."[2] In Israel, anointing marked someone as consecrated for divine service, often with oil poured over their head.[3] John 1:41 describes Andrew telling his brother Simon Peter, "We have found the Messiah" (which is translated "the Christ"), he was declaring that Jesus is the promised Anointed One. In the Old Testament scriptures, the Messiah was a religious leader who was believed to be anointed by God and sent to redeem and save humanity from sin and bring about God's kingdom on earth.

The disciples' question in Acts 1:6—"Lord, are you restoring the kingdom to Israel at this time?"—perfectly captures Israel's long-standing expectation for a Messiah rooted in God's ancient promises. Even after the resurrection, they still viewed the Messiah's mission primarily in political and national terms. Their question wasn't random—it was anchored in something every first-century Jew would have known: God's covenant with David.

Jewish Messianic Expectation & the Davidic Covenant

In 2 Samuel 7:16, God made a direct promise to King David: *"Your house and kingdom will endure before me forever, and your throne*

---

2. Gerard Van Groningen, "Messiah" in *Evangelical Dictionary of Biblical Theology*, electronic ed., Baker Reference Library (Grand Rapids: Baker Book House, 1996), 523.

3. Walter A. Elwell and Barry J. Beitzel, "Messiah," in *Baker Encyclopedia of the Bible* (Grand Rapids, MI: Baker Book House, 1988), 1446.

will be established forever." This is what theologians call the Davidic Covenant, an unconditional promise that God would establish an everlasting dynasty through one of David's descendants who would sit on his throne forever. In other words, Israel's hope for a coming Messiah wasn't built on wishful thinking—it was grounded in a divine covenant.

Other Old Testament passages like 2 Samuel 22:48-51 and Jeremiah 33:14-26 reinforced this expectation, describing a future ruler from David's line who would reign with justice and righteousness over all the earth.[4] As Elwell and Beitzel note, orthodox rabbi's never lacked conjecture about the Messiah's identity and that at one time they applied no less than 456 passages of Scripture to his person and salvation.[5] For many Jews living under Roman oppression, this Messiah was expected to be a political liberator—an earthly king who would overthrow their enemies and restore Israel's glory. Yet the gospel reveals that Jesus fulfilled those promises in a far greater way—by establishing a kingdom that is both spiritual and eternal.

The Protoevangelium (Gen. 3:15)

The hope for a Messiah was not merely for a human ruler but for the fulfillment of the very first messianic prophecy found in Genesis 3:15: *"I will put hostility between you and the woman, and between your offspring and her offspring. He will strike your head, and you will strike his heel."*

This passage is known as the protoevangelium, meaning "the first gospel." It is the earliest announcement of God's redemptive plan —

---

4. Elwell and Beitzel, *Baker Encyclopedia of the Bible*, 1446.

5. Ibid, 1446

the first hint that a Deliverer would come to defeat evil at its source. The wording in Hebrew emphasizes certainty: a male descendant ("He") will one day crush the serpent's head, symbolizing a decisive victory over Satan.[6] The serpent will inflict harm by striking the heel, but the ultimate blow will belong to the woman's seed.

Many scholars and believers recognize in this prophecy the foreshadowing of Christ's death and resurrection — the moment when Jesus, through the cross, turned what looked like defeat into victory (1 Cor. 15:55–57). This same victory will be completed in the final judgment (Rev. 12:7–10; 20:7–10).[7] Through this lens, we see why the incarnation matters so deeply: God entered the world in human flesh to fulfill a promise that began in Eden. Humanity had been struggling against sin since that first fall, unable to overcome it—until God Himself entered the fight. The incarnation was Heaven's intervention, when the Almighty stepped into the conflict to secure the victory promised from the beginning.

By the time of Jesus' birth, Jews living under Roman rule were not concerned with predicting a specific *date* for the Messiah's arrival — they were longing for the *event* itself. The incarnation was the fulfillment of that ancient promise: the moment when the seed of the woman finally entered history.

Old Testament Prophecies of the Incarnation

---

6. Robert D. Bergen, "Genesis," in *CSB Study Bible: Notes*, ed. Edwin A. Blum and Trevin Wax (Nashville, TN: Holman Bible Publishers, 2017), 11.

7. Biblical Studies Press, *The NET Bible First Edition Notes* (Biblical Studies Press, 2006), Ge 3:15.

DEBUNKING THE PAGAN ROOTS OF CHRISTMAS

Among the Old Testament prophecies that point to the incarnation, none is more central than Isaiah 7:14: *"Therefore, the Lord himself will give you a sign: See, the virgin will conceive, have a son, and name him Immanuel."*

Critics often argue that this verse doesn't truly predict a virgin birth because the Hebrew word *'almāh'* means "young woman," not "virgin." Yet this objection overlooks two crucial facts. First, in ancient Israelite culture, a *young unmarried woman* was assumed to be a virgin. The term *'almāh'* never refers to a non-virgin anywhere in Scripture (see Gen 24:43; Exod 2:8; Prov 30:19). Another Hebrew term, *bĕtûlāh*, is often translated "virgin," but even that word can describe a married or betrothed woman (Joel 1:8). Thus Isaiah's choice of *'almāh'*—which always denotes an unmarried girl—actually communicates the concept of virginity more precisely within that cultural setting.

Second, when Jewish scholars translated the Hebrew Scriptures into Greek around 200 B.C. (the Septuagint), they rendered *'almāh'* as *parthenos*, a word that unambiguously means "virgin." This demonstrates that long before the birth of Jesus, Jewish interpreters themselves understood Isaiah 7:14 as foretelling a miraculous conception, not merely the birth of a child to a young woman. When Matthew cites Isaiah's prophecy (Matt 1:23), he is not redefining the text but confirming the interpretation already embedded in the Jewish Bible of his day.

The significance of Isaiah 7:14 cannot be overstated: from the earliest pages of Scripture, God was revealing His plan to dwell among His people as *Immanuel*—"God with us." The incarnation was not an unexpected miracle but the long-promised fulfillment of this prophetic sign. Isaiah would later expand upon this promise, revealing not only the miraculous nature of the Messiah's birth but also His divine identity and eternal reign. What began as a sign to King Ahaz in Isaiah 7 becomes, by Isaiah 9, a revelation to the entire world: the promised child is none other than God Himself, come to rule with justice and peace.

Another well-known prophecy appears in Isaiah 9:6: *"For a child will be born for us, a son will be given to us, and the government will be on his shoulders. He will be named Wonderful Counselor, Mighty God, Eternal Father, Prince of Peace."*

In this single verse, Isaiah captures both the humanity and divinity of the Messiah. "A child will be born" speaks of His human birth; "a son will be given" points to His divine preexistence—the eternal Son of God entering time and space.[8] The title *Mighty God* leaves no ambiguity about His divinity, affirming that the promised child is none other than God Himself.

Some readers misunderstand the title *Eternal Father*, assuming it confuses the Messiah with God the Father, but the phrase is actually what we call a Hebrew idiom—a figure of speech where the words don't literally mean what they appear to say. For instance, when someone says, "break a leg," they don't mean it literally; it's a way of wishing someone good luck. In the same way, "Eternal Father" doesn't mean that the Son *is* the Father within the Trinity. Instead, it describes the Messiah's relationship to time, not His relationship within the Godhead.

Just as "the Ancient of Days" in Daniel 7 portrays God's eternal rule—and is clearly distinct from the Son of Man, who receives dominion from Him—"Eternal Father" identifies the Messiah as the

---

8. Warren W. Wiersbe, *Be Comforted*, "Be" Commentary Series (Wheaton, IL: Victor Books, 1996), 37.

source and sustainer of eternity: the Father, or originator, of everlasting life for His people.

Scripture uses "father" in this figurative sense in several places: the "father of rain" (Job 38:28), the "father of lies" (John 8:44), and the "Father of mercies" (2 Cor 1:3 KJV; Eph 1:17 KJV).[9] Isaiah's prophecy therefore presents a ruler who is both infinitely powerful and intimately personal—a Wonderful Counselor, a Mighty God, and the Prince of Peace whose kingdom will have no end. This is the very heart of the incarnation: the eternal God stepping into human history to reign, redeem, and restore.

Having revealed both the miraculous birth and divine identity of the coming Messiah, God did not leave His people guessing about where this promised ruler would enter history. Through another prophet, Micah, the Lord narrowed the focus even further—identifying not only the family line but the very town where the eternal King would be born. What Isaiah proclaimed about *who* the Messiah would be, Micah declared about *where* He would appear.

Micah's Geographical Precision

One of the most specific prophecies concerning the Messiah's coming is found in Micah 5:2: *"Bethlehem Ephrathah, you are small among the clans of Judah; one will come from you to be ruler over Israel for me. His origin is from antiquity, from ancient times."*

---

[9]. James M. Freeman and Harold J. Chadwick, *Manners & Customs of the Bible* (North Brunswick, NJ: Bridge-Logos Publishers, 1998), 7.

This passage is a salvation oracle (message from deity to humans) promising deliverance from the Assyrians and a return from exile.[10] The humiliation Israel's leaders faced (Mic. 5:1) would one day be overturned in what I like to call the ultimate uno-reverse—God flipping the script entirely as a new ruler arises from an unlikely place: Bethlehem.

Ephrathah was the ancient name for Bethlehem and also the name of the surrounding district (see Gen. 35:16, 19; 48:7; Ruth 4:11).[11] The name itself came from *Ephrath*, one of the clans that made up the tribe of Judah (Ruth 1:2).[12] David's family belonged to this clan (1 Sam. 17:12), which is why Micah's prophecy deliberately connects Bethlehem—the "city of David"—to the future ruler who would come from David's line.

Some interpreters assume that the phrase *"His origin is from antiquity, from ancient times"* speaks directly of the Messiah's divinity. While that idea harmonizes with the eternal nature of Christ, the immediate context points to the long-established Davidic dynasty. By the time Micah prophesied in the eighth century B.C., Judah's kings had ruled for roughly three hundred years, all descendants of David. Micah's message was clear: the promised ruler would come from that same ancient royal line — a lineage that God Himself had

---

10. Richard D. Patterson and Andrew E. Hill, *Cornerstone Biblical Commentary, Vol 10: Minor Prophets, Hosea–Malachi* (Carol Stream, IL: Tyndale House Publishers, 2008), 329.

11. Tokunboh Adeyemo, *Africa Bible Commentary* (Nairobi, Kenya; Grand Rapids, MI: WordAlive Publishers; Zondervan, 2006), 1080.

12. David J. Clark and Norm Mundhenk, *A Translator's Handbook on the Book of Micah*, UBS Handbook Series (London; New York: United Bible Societies, 1982), 206.

ordained.[13] Yet prophecy often carries layers of fulfillment. What was historically true of David's dynasty finds its ultimate and divine fulfillment in Jesus—the eternal Son of God—born in the very town that once produced Israel's shepherd king. God's promise narrowed from a covenant, to a tribe, to a family, and finally to a place—Bethlehem—showing that the incarnation was no coincidence but a precise act of divine orchestration.

The Righteous Branch: The Divine King of David's Line

The final Old Testament prophecy we'll examine comes from Jeremiah 23:5–6, where the Lord declares, *"Look, the days are coming... when I will raise up a Righteous Branch for David. He will reign wisely as king and administer justice and righteousness in the land. In his days Judah will be saved, and Israel will dwell securely. This is the name he will be called: The LORD Is Our Righteousness."*

What's remarkable is that this coming ruler—clearly described as a human descendant of David—is identified by the divine name *YHWH* (*Yahweh*), the same sacred name used more than 6,000 times in the Old Testament to refer to God alone. Jeremiah's prophecy therefore reveals something astounding: the Messiah who would one day sit on David's throne would not only reign as a man but would bear the very name of God Himself.

The title *"The LORD Is Our Righteousness" (YHWH Tsidkenu)* anticipates the redemptive work of Christ, who would become righteousness on behalf of His people (2 Cor. 5:21). In Him, the covenant promises made to David reach their ultimate fulfillment. The eternal

---

13. Clark and Mundhenk, *A Translator's Handbook on the Book of Micah*, 207.

God took on human flesh to be both the King who rules and the Savior who redeems.

The Old Testament doesn't merely foretell the coming of a Messiah—it reveals the promise of a divine Messiah: one born of a woman, descended from David, yet bearing the very name *YHWH*. The incarnation is not a New Testament invention but the fulfillment of God's ancient promise to dwell with His people in person.

Every prophecy—from Isaiah's virgin birth, to Micah's humble Bethlehem, to Jeremiah's Righteous Branch—converges on one reality: God Himself came near. What Israel longed for in promise, we now celebrate in fulfillment—the eternal Word made flesh, dwelling among us.

The Incarnation Is Wild

I encourage you to pause and reread the previous line before continuing. Reflect on what it truly means: Yahweh, the Holy One of Israel, dwelled... lived... tabernacled... with human beings—as a human being. As I write these words, I'm overwhelmed by the weight of that reality. Any attempt to fully describe it feels inadequate, so I'll borrow the words of someone who captured it perfectly.

On December 22, 2022, author and speaker Jackie Hill Perry posted a message to her verified Instagram account titled *"The Incarnation Is Wild."* In it, she powerfully summarized what the prophets could only glimpse:

> Moses couldn't come near the bush. Isaiah could see God's robe filling the temple but he could not see his face. Israel couldn't come near the mountain. Uzzah simply placed his hand on the ark and God's wrath

came out in judgment killing him. The priest could only go into God's presence once a year and even then, there was a constant threat from death. From Genesis to Malachi is the story of people not being able to freely come near to God because of His holiness and their sin, but the glory of the incarnation is that God Himself has come near to us. For Jesus to be swaddled, God had to be...touched. For the shepherds to praise God for the Savior that was born, God had to be...seen. The Holy, Holy, Holy God that Isaiah saw on the throne condescended, taking on human flesh, living with, eating with, speaking with, and touching, sinners. This is why He is called Immanuel, God with us. [14]

This...family, is what Christmas is about. Have we become so familiar with the Christmas story that we are desensitized to its spiritual significance? God is with us. In Christianity, the incarnation means that the eternal, transcendent, personal God became fully human in the person of Jesus the Christ (Jn. 1:14; Phil. 2:6-8). To be clear, God did not *appear* as a human but truly *became* human while fully retaining divinity. This concept of incarnation is unparalleled in world religions. For God to live among, suffer with, and die for his own creation, is truly wild. No other deity in any religion in the world makes this claim.

---

14. Jackie Hill Perry, "The Incarnation Is Wild," video post, *Instagram*, December 22, 2022, https://www.instagram.com/jackiehillperry/.

They Not Like Us

Let's be clear—the incarnation isn't just unique; it's unmatched. No other faith in the world makes the same claim Christianity does: that the eternal God stepped into human history, took on flesh, and lived among His creation. Every other system either stops short of that truth or runs in the opposite direction.

In Hinduism, deities like Vishnu appear in various forms such as Krishna or Rama. These avatars are often called "incarnations," but they are temporary manifestations or mythological representations—not permanent unions of divine and human nature. They happen within a cycle of time, not a specific moment in history. By contrast, the incarnation of Jesus was a real event in space and time, with a clear purpose: to reconcile mankind to God. Hinduism's goal is *moksha*—the liberation of the soul from the cycle of rebirth—not redemption through a Savior.[15]

In Greek and Roman mythology, gods like Zeus, Hermes, and Apollo sometimes appear in human form or have relationships with humans, but always in disguise. They pretend to be human; they don't *become* human. These are divine impersonations, not incarnations. Similarly, Egyptian mythology viewed the pharaohs as divine or semi-divine, but that's the opposite process—humans becoming gods, not God becoming man.

Buddhism has no personal Creator-God. "Buddha" is not a name but a title meaning "the awakened one."[16] Siddhartha Gautama—the

---

15. Ron Geaves, "Moksha (1)," in *Continuum Glossary of Religious Terms* (London; New York: Continuum, 2002), 251.

16. Mark Water, ed., *AMG's Encyclopedia of World Religions, Cults & the Occult: Tough Questions, Clear Answers* (AMG Publishers, 2006), 215.

DEBUNKING THE PAGAN ROOTS OF CHRISTMAS 17

historical Buddha—was an enlightened man, not a deity. Later Buddhist traditions introduced celestial Buddhas, but these are manifestations of enlightenment, not divine beings taking on flesh. Even revered figures like the Dalai Lama are viewed as reincarnations of compassion, not incarnations of deity.[17]

In Islam, the idea of God becoming human is explicitly denied. This is one of the central convictions of *tawhid*—the absolute oneness of Allah. To associate any partner or likeness with God is the gravest sin, called *shirk*. The Qur'an is emphatic: *"Say, 'He is Allah, [who is] One, Allah, the Eternal Refuge. He neither begets nor is born, nor is there to Him any equivalent'"* (Qur'an, Al-Ikhlāṣ 112:1–4, trans. Talal Itani). In a direct rejection of Christian belief, the Qur'an warns:

> O People of the Book! Do not go to extremes regarding your faith; say nothing about Allah except the truth. The Messiah, Jesus, son of Mary, was no more than a messenger of Allah and the fulfilment of His Word through Mary and a spirit ▫created by a command▫ from Him. So believe in Allah and His messengers and do not say, "Trinity." Stop!—for your own good. Allah is only One God. Glory be to Him! He is far above having a son! (*Qur'an*, An-Nisā' 4:171, trans. M. A. S. Abdel Haleem).

As these examples show, while other religions tell stories of gods visiting, disguising, or enlightening, only Christianity declares that the eternal God literally became human—and that He did so not as myth,

---

17. Ron Geaves, "Dalai Lama," *Continuum Glossary of Religious Terms*, 87.

metaphor, or momentary manifestation, but as verifiable history. The Word became flesh and dwelt among us (John 1:14).

That's why I say, *they not like us*. Every other system describes humanity reaching for God; Christianity reveals God reaching for humanity. That's what makes the incarnation—and Christmas itself—utterly unique.

Can I Get A Witness?

The Bible goes to great lengths to demonstrate how important and overwhelming the miracle of the incarnation was. C.S. Lewis once observed:

The central miracle asserted by Christians is the incarnation. They say that God became man. Every other miracle prepares for this, or exhibits this, or results from this. Just as every natural event is the manifestation at a particular place and moment in nature's total character, so every particular Christian miracle manifests at a particular place and moment the character and significance of the incarnation.[18]

What Lewis captures so brilliantly is that the Incarnation is the foundation of every miracle. The miracles of Scripture are not random interruptions in nature; they're revelations of God's nature. Each one either *prepares for*, *reveals*, or *results from* the miracle of God becoming man.

Just as we learn what nature is like by studying the world around us, we learn what God is like by studying the miracles of Jesus. The Incarnation is proof that the God who created the world also stepped into the world—showing that divine power is not distant, but personal, present, and purposeful.

---

18. C. S. Lewis, *Miracles* (London, England: HarperCollins, 1998), 173.

When God decided to step into human history, heaven and earth both showed up to testify. Angels announced it. Shepherds witnessed it. Prophets proclaimed it. And wise men traveled across nations to worship it. The arrival of Jesus didn't just happen; it was *witnessed, worshiped, and verified.*

In his gospel account, Luke records that while shepherds were keeping watch in the fields near Bethlehem, *"an angel of the Lord stood before them and proclaimed, 'Today in the city of David a Savior was born for you, who is the Messiah, the Lord'"* (Luke 2:11 CSB).

The Heavenly Choir's Diss Track

Heaven couldn't hold its joy. *"Suddenly there was a multitude of the heavenly host with the angel, praising God and saying: Glory to God in the highest heaven, and peace on earth to people he favors!"* (Luke 2:13–14 CSB). Notice what's happening here: one angel announces, but an army of angels arrives. They weren't celebrating from heaven; Luke says they came down to earth to celebrate—because this wasn't just any child's birth. This was the Savior's arrival, the moment when God stepped into flesh. Even the angels understood that this was not a birthday party—it was the miracle of the Incarnation.

Luke's description also carries a deeper message. The angels declare Jesus as *"Savior"* and *"Lord."* In the Greek Septuagint,[19] the word *kurios* (Lord) was used to translate *YHWH*—the sacred, personal name of God Himself.[20] Luke is boldly identifying this child not only as Messiah but as God in human form.

And then comes the polemic. A *polemical statement* is a direct, verbal challenge to a competing idea—or as we'd say today, a "diss track." Hip-hop culture is known for artists dropping "diss tracks" to prove who's really on top. In the same way, Luke's use of *"good news," "Savior,"* and *"Lord"* hits like a holy diss track aimed at the Roman Empire's false gospel.[21] In the first century, these very titles were used to celebrate Caesar Augustus, who was hailed as the world's "savior" bringing "peace" to all people.[22] Luke flips that narrative entirely. Heaven's chorus declares that the real peace doesn't come from an emperor's empire, but from the Eternal King's incarnation. This wasn't a celebration of a date—it was the announcement of

---

19. The name Septuagint comes from the Latin *septuaginta,* meaning "seventy." It was a Koine Greek translation of the Hebrew Old Testament. The designation "seventy" is given to this group of writings because, according to ancient tradition, about seventy (or in some versions of the story, seventy-two) Jewish rabbis, secluded from one another and under divine inspiration, all produced identical Greek translations of the Torah from Hebrew. Rick Mansfield, "Best Septuagint (LXX) Translations," *Logos* (blog), September 2, 2025, https://www.logos.com/grow/best-septuagint-lxx-translations/#:~:text=The%20origins%20and%20name%20of,sincerely%20believed%20in%20ancient%20times.

20. Allison A. Trites, William J. Larkin, *Cornerstone Biblical Commentary, Vol 12: The Gospel of Luke and Acts* (Carol Stream, IL: Tyndale House Publishers, 2006), 55.

21. Craig S. Keener, *The IVP Bible Background Commentary: New Testament* (Downers Grove, IL: InterVarsity Press, 1993), Lk 2:10–12.

22. Keener, *The IVP Bible Background Commentary: New Testament,* Lk 2:13-14.

a Deliverer. Heaven's army came down to declare that peace had a person, and His name was Jesus.

The Shepherds: Ordinary Men, Extraordinary Moment

In response to the angels' announcement, the shepherds said to one another, *"Let's go straight to Bethlehem and see what has happened, which the Lord has made known to us"* (Luke 2:15 CSB). They hurried into town, found the baby lying in a manger, and spread the news of what the angels had said. Luke tells us, *"All who heard it were amazed at what the shepherds said to them"* (v.18). When they returned to their flocks, they were *"glorifying and praising God for all the things they had seen and heard, which were just as they had been told"* (v.20).

The angels had proclaimed, and now the shepherds praised. Both heaven and earth rejoiced together over the same truth—the miracle of the Incarnation. The shepherds weren't celebrating a *when*; they were celebrating a *who*.

Simeon: The Patient Prophet

Forty days later, after Mary's purification was complete (Lev. 12:3–4), she and Joseph brought Jesus to Jerusalem to dedicate Him to the Lord, as commanded in Exodus 13:2 (Luke 2:22–23). There they met a man named Simeon, described as *"righteous and devout,"* who was *"looking forward to Israel's consolation"* (v.25). That word *consolation* refers to comfort or deliverance—the hope that God would once again intervene for His people (see Isa. 49:13; 51:3; 52:9; 66:13).[23] Therefore, what Luke describes is a messianic expectation. God had

---

23. Keener, *The IVP Bible Background Commentary: New Testament*, Lk 2:25–26.

promised Simeon that he would not die before seeing the Messiah. Guided by the Spirit, he entered the temple as Jesus arrived. Taking Him in his arms, he praised God:

Now, Master, you can dismiss your servant in peace, as you promised. For my eyes have seen your salvation. You have prepared it in the presence of all peoples— a light for revelation to the Gentiles[24] and glory to your people Israel. His father and mother were amazed at what was being said about him. (Luk 2:29-33 CSB)

Simeon's song is pure satisfaction. He had waited his whole life for this moment, and now he held the fulfillment of every prophecy in his arms. The long-expected Messiah had come—not just for Israel, but for the world.

Anna: The Faithful Witness

At that very moment, a prophetess named Anna approached. She was *"a widow of eighty-four years... who did not leave the temple, serving God night and day with fasting and prayers"* (vv.36–37). When she saw Jesus, she immediately began giving thanks to God and *"spoke about him to all who were looking forward to the redemption of Jerusalem"* (v.38).

Simeon sang about God's salvation; Anna spoke about God's redemption. Both recognized what God was doing. And just like

---

[24]. Luke 2:32 is an excellent verse for apologetics against Hebrew Israelites, a heretical sect who claim misinterpret passages such as Deut. 28:68 as speaking to the transatlantic slave trade. They assert that salvation is only available for ethnic Israelites. Lk 2:32 explicitly states that Jesus' life was a revelation to the Gentiles *and* to Israel. This refutes their claim that Gentiles in the NT refers to Israelites from the northern kingdom who were scattered. For more information, see Dr. Eric Mason's "Urban Apologetics, Vol. 1: Restoring Black Dignity With The Gospel."

the shepherds before them, they didn't focus on the timing of His birth—they rejoiced in the truth of His presence.

Four scenes. Four witnesses. One message. Heaven, shepherds, Simeon, and Anna all responded the same way—with praise, proclamation, and pure joy. The event, not the date, moved them to worship.

The Wise Men: Seekers From The East

Our final witnesses appear in Matthew's Gospel. While this isn't the place for a deep dive into authorship, it's worth noting that the early Church consistently affirmed that Matthew—the former tax collector turned disciple—wrote this account. The testimony of Church Fathers like Papias, Irenaeus, and Origen was unanimous, and that tradition went virtually unchallenged for nearly two thousand years.[25]

Matthew tells us that *"wise men from the east arrived in Jerusalem, saying, 'Where is he who has been born king of the Jews? For we saw his star at its rising and have come to worship him'"* (Matt. 2:1–2 CSB). These "wise men," or *magi*, (AMP, LSB, NASB, NIV, etc.) refer to the learned court advisers of Mesopotamia or Persia whose work involved studying ancient and sacred texts, as well as watching for movements of planets and stars that might be interpreted as divine messages.[26] The historian Herodotus describes the Magi as Zoroastrian priests

---

25. For Papias, see Eusebius, *Church History* 3.39.16, where Papias is cited as referring to Matthew compiling the "sayings" of Jesus. For Irenaeus, see *Against Heresies* 3.1.1, where he identifies Matthew as the author of the first Gospel and affirms the traditional authorship of the gospels of Mark, Luke, and John. For Origen, see Eusebius, *Church History* 6.25.4, where Origen also confirms the traditional authorship of all four gospel authors as well.

26. Mark Krause, "Wise Men, Magi," in *The Lexham Bible Dictionary*, ed. John D. Barry et al. (Bellingham, WA: Lexham Press, 2016).

who interpreted the movements of the heavens as messages from the divine.[27]

Contrary to popular tradition, Matthew never tells us there were three wise men; the number comes from the three gifts presented to Jesus.[28] But what matters more is *who* these men were—Gentile scholars from far-off nations who recognized what Israel had been waiting for. They weren't just seeking a king; they were seeking the King.

When their inquiry reached King Herod, *"he was deeply disturbed, and all Jerusalem with him"* (v.3). And for good reason. Matthew—himself a Jewish writer—uses intentional language that hits like another polemical "diss track." The Magi's question—*"Where is he who has been born king of the Jews?"*—was a direct threat to Herod's ego and empire. "King of the Jews" was Herod's self-appointed title,[29] yet he was not Jewish by blood. He was an Idumean[30] – a Greek name given to people from Idumea, a region south of Judea. The Idumeans were the descendants of Esau, the twin brother of the patriarch Jacob. Idumeans were previously known as Edomites. During the 2nd century BCE, the Jewish Hasmonean ruler John Hyrcanus conquered Idumea and forcibly converted the

---

27. Walter A. Elwell and Barry J. Beitzel, https://ref.ly/logosres/bkrencbib?ref=Page.p+2154&off=503&ctx=magi+were+therefore+~concerned+with+what+ in *Baker Encyclopedia of the Bible* (Grand Rapids, MI: Baker Book House, 1988), 2154.

28. Some traditions name the wise men as Melchior, Caspar, and Balthazar. Some Eastern Christian traditions place the number of wise men at 12. Krause, "Wise Men, Magi," under *Number* and *Names*

29. Craig S. Keener, *Matthew*, vol. 1, The IVP New Testament Commentary Series (Downers Grove, IL: InterVarsity Press, 1997), Mt 2:1–12.

30. Josephus, *The Jewish War*, trans. G. A. Williamson, rev. E. Mary Smallwood (New York: Penguin Books, 1981), 1.123, 313

Idumeans into Judaism and incorporated them into the Jewish nation. According to Jewish law (Deut. 17:15), he wasn't even eligible to be king. So imagine being a Jew living in the first century, having a Jewish convert who is forbidden to be king according to Jewish law (Deut. 17:15) as your leader. Worst of all his position as Jewish king was given to him by through political manipulation by the Romans – the very empire oppressing God's people.[31] Herod's throne was a Roman favor, not a divine appointment.

So while the wise men unknowingly struck a nerve, Matthew intentionally amplified it. He's showing his readers that even Gentile scholars recognized the true King while Israel's counterfeit king trembled. What the Magi asked in innocence, Matthew recorded with precision — a direct challenge to the empire's false gospel and a declaration that Israel's rightful ruler had finally arrived.

Herod was responsible for refurbishing the Jewish temple in Jerusalem, but he also built three temples to the first Roman Emperor, Caesar Augustus.[32] Josephus recorded multiple stories of Herod's harsh treatment of the Jews[33] and it was the fear of potential usurpers[34] that caused Herod to order the massacre of male children two years and under in and around Bethlehem (Matt. 2:16).

---

31. John G. Butler, *Analytical Bible Expositor: Matthew* (Clinton, IA: LBC Publications, 2008), 33.

32. Benjamin A. Foreman, "Matthew's Birth Narrative," in *Lexham Geographic Commentary on the Gospels*, ed. Barry J. Beitzel and Kristopher A. Lyle, Lexham Geographic Commentary (Bellingham, WA: Lexham Press, 2016), 23.

33. Josephus, *The Antiquities of the Jews*, trans. G. A. Williamson, rev. E. Mary Smallwood (New York: Penguin Books, 1981), 17.191.

34. Foreman, "Matthew's Birth Narrative," 23.

Matthew tells us Herod consulted the chief priests and scribes, who confirmed that the Messiah was to be born in Bethlehem (vv.4–6). He sent the Magi to find the child, pretending he wanted to worship Him, though in reality he wanted to kill Him.

The star reappeared, leading the Magi to the place where Jesus and His family were staying. When they saw the star stop, they were *"overwhelmed with joy"* (v.10). These Gentile scholars—men raised in polytheistic systems—fell to their knees before a Jewish child and worshiped Him.

Note that this story happens a considerable amount of time after the events of Luke 2. Judging from Herod's decree impacting children two years and under and the use of the Greek word for child[35] in vv. 9–11, Jesus would have been a toddler and not a newborn. Even so, the Magi didn't care about *when* He was born—they cared about *why* He was born. Even their gifts revealed their recognition of Jesus' identity:

- Gold recognized that Jesus was King.

- Frankincense represented reverence of His deity

- Myrrh represents human sorrows and the ability to offer pain and repentance to God.[36] There is also the belief that myrrh prophetically foretold His death.[37]

---

35. Matthew uses the Greek *paidion* – *"young child"* in vv.9–11 rather than *brephos (βρέφος)*, which means *"infant"* or *"newborn"* which Luke used for the baby in the manger (Luke 2:12,16).

36. Joseph S. Exell, *The Biblical Illustrator: Matthew* (Grand Rapids, MI: Baker Book House, 1952), 11.

37. David Turner and Darrell L. Bock, *Cornerstone Biblical Commentary, Vol 11: Matthew and Mark* (Carol Stream, IL: Tyndale House Publishers, 2005), 49.

The Magi traveled hundreds of miles and many months for one reason—to worship. They celebrated not a date, but a divine arrival. Gentiles from the East bowing before the Messiah of Israel was God's way of announcing that the Savior of the world had come.

Heaven witnessed it. Earth witnessed it. The nations witnessed it. Angels announced it, shepherds proclaimed it, Simeon and Anna praised it, and wise men traveled across continents to worship it. Five witnesses. One message. The Incarnation is worth celebrating.

If the inspired writers of Scripture took the time to record these celebrations, why shouldn't we? The angels filled the skies with praise. The shepherds filled Bethlehem with testimony. Simeon and Anna filled the temple with worship. And the Magi filled their hands with gifts. Each responded to the same reality—that God had come near. They weren't honoring a date; they were adoring a Deliverer.

Some reject the celebration of Christmas because they misunderstand its meaning. But when we celebrate the birth of Christ, we're not bowing to tradition—we're responding to revelation. The Bible doesn't command the celebration of the Incarnation, but it clearly commends it by example. Worship, after all, isn't limited to a calendar; it's the natural response to divine visitation. Celebration is not compromise; it is confession — a declaration that God has kept His promise.

My prayer is that as you read this chapter, your heart has been stirred to see Christmas for what it truly is: the celebration of the moment when Heaven invaded earth, eternity entered time, and the Word became flesh. In the chapters ahead, we'll examine the historical evidence to show that this holy day has never been rooted in paganism, but in prophecy fulfilled.

Like the Bereans in Acts 17, search the Scriptures and weigh the evidence for yourself. I'm confident you'll find what they found—that the only conclusion possible is this: Christmas was never borrowed from the pagans; it was birthed from the promise of God.

3

THE DATE OF DECEMBER 25: BIBLICAL AND HISTORICAL ROOTS

If Chapter 1 laid the theological foundation for the celebration of Christmas, this chapter turns our attention to the historical question that often fuels controversy: *Why December 25?*

For centuries, skeptics have claimed that Christian's "stole" this date from pagan festivals—borrowing from celebrations like Saturnalia or Sol Invictus and rebranding them as the birth of Jesus. It's one of the most common objections you'll encounter in conversations about Christmas, and it sounds convincing—until you actually look at the evidence.

The truth is that December 25 wasn't chosen to Imitate paganism; It was chosen to illustrate prophecy and celebrate theology. Early Christians didn't borrow from Rome's festivals—they built on God's timeline. And as we'll see, both Scripture and early church history point to far deeper reasons for the date than cultural coincidence.

Before we trace how December 25 came to be recognized as the celebration of Christ's birth, we'll examine the ancient calendars, historical records, and theological reasoning that shaped the early church's choice. Because understanding the *when* of Christmas is not just about a date in history—it's about seeing how divine design intersects with human time.

The Eastern and Western Church in Early Christianity

In the first centuries of Christianity, distinct Eastern and Western church traditions developed due to cultural and linguistic divisions within the Roman Empire. The Eastern regions (like Constantinople, Antioch, and Alexandria) were Greek-speaking, while the Western regions (centered on Rome) used Latin. This East-West divide shaped how Christians worshiped, thought, and celebrated key events in Christ's life. Though united in faith, the two sides expressed their devotion differently, including how and when they celebrated the Incarnation of Christ. These early distinctions set the stage for different feast day traditions, including Epiphany and eventually Christmas.

Julian vs. Gregorian Calendars: Why Dates Differ

Early Christians used the Julian calendar, introduced by Julius Caesar. It assumed a year was 365.25 days long, which was slightly off. Over centuries, this small error added up, causing the calendar to drift from the actual solar year.

To fix this, Pope Gregory XIII introduced the Gregorian calendar in 1582. It dropped 10 days and adjusted leap years. Western Europe adopted this change, but many Eastern Orthodox churches did not. As a result, Eastern churches using the Julian calendar now celebrate key feasts 13 days later than Western churches. That's why many Orthodox Christians observe Christmas on January 7 (which is December 25 on the Julian calendar) and Epiphany on January

19 (Julian January 6). The difference isn't about theology, but about which calendar is used.

Epiphany: The First Feast Of The Incarnation

Before there was Christmas, many Christians celebrated the Incarnation at a feast called Epiphany. The word "Epiphany" means "appearance" or "manifestation."[1] Celebrated on January 6, it celebrates the manifestation of Christ to the Gentiles which is seen in the coming of the Maji to see Jesus (Matt. 2:1-12). The 12 days between Christmas and Epiphany is where we get the "Twelve Days of Christmas."[2]

In the East, Epiphany (often called Theophany) highlighted Jesus's baptism in the Jordan River—when the Father's voice, the Spirit's dove, and the Son in the water all revealed the Trinity. In the West, Epiphany focused on the visit of the Magi, showing that Christ had come for the whole world, not just the Jews.

In the early centuries, some churches even celebrated Christ's birth on January 6 as part of Epiphany. Over time, though, the Western Church introduced a separate feast for the Nativity on December 25. This new celebration gradually spread eastward. By the late 4th and early 5th centuries, many churches celebrated both: December 25 as Christ's birth and January 6 as His baptism or the visit of the Magi. This two-part celebration deepened the churches' reverence. Christmas honors the mystery of God made flesh; Epiphany honors how that mystery was revealed to the world. Together, they proclaim that the Word was made flesh and made known to all nations.

---

1. Fred A. Grissom, "Epiphany," in *Holman Illustrated Bible Dictionary*, ed. Chad Brand et al. (Nashville, TN: Holman Bible Publishers, 2003), 501.

2. Grisson, "Epiphany," 501.

A Tale of Two Theories

There are two main schools of thought that attempt to explain why December 25th was adopted by early Christians — the *History of Religions* hypothesis and the *Calculation (or Computation) Hypothesis*. The *History of Religions hypothesis was first proposed by Hermann Usener in 1889.*[3] This theory is often called the *pagan-substitution theory* because it suggests that December 25 was influenced by—or intended to replace—pagan feast days celebrated around that same time, such as *Dies Natalis Solis Invicti* (commonly called *Sol Invictus*), the "Feast of the Unconquered Sun.[4] We will examine this claim in greater detail in subsequent chapters.

Supporters of this theory often point to ancient calendars and writings that appear to connect the winter solstice with pagan celebrations. For example, some have claimed that during the reign of Amenemhet I—the founder of Egypt's Twelfth Dynasty (1991–1962 B.C.)—the Egyptians observed the winter solstice on a date that would later correspond to January 6.[5] Epiphanius of Salamis (315-403) also described a festival held in honor of the god Aeon, said to have been born to the virgin Core on that same date:

---

3. Hermann Usener, *Das Weihnachtsfest* [*The Christmas Feast*] (Bonn: Cohen, 1889), discussed in Timothy Larsen, ed., *The Oxford Handbook of Christmas* (London: Oxford University Press, 2020), 42–43.

4. Timothy Larsen, ed., *The Oxford Handbook of Christmas* (London, England: Oxford University Press, 2020), 4.

5. Eduard Norden, *Die Geburt des Kindes* [*The Birth of the Child*] (Leipzig: Teubner, 1924), discussed in Timothy Larsen, ed., *The Oxford Handbook of Christmas* (London: Oxford University Press, 2020), 4.

DEBUNKING THE PAGAN ROOTS OF CHRISTMAS

> At Alexandria, in the Coreum, as they call it, it is a very large temple, the shrine of Core. They stay up all night singing hymns to the idol with a flute accompaniment. And when they have concluded their nightlong vigil torchbearers descend into an underground shrine after cockcrow and bring up a wooden image which is seated naked [on] a litter. It has a sign of the cross inlaid with gold on its forehead, two other such signs, [one] actually [on each of] its two knees—altogether five signs with a gold impress. And they carry the image itself seven times round the innermost shrine with flutes, tambourines and hymns, hold a feast, and take it back down to its place underground. And when you ask them what this mystery means they reply that today at this hour Core—that is, the virgin—gave birth to Aeon.[6]

The History of Religions hypothesis uses sources like these to argue that early Christians borrowed or adapted pagan themes. For more than sixty years this idea dominated scholarly discussion[7]—until it was effectively challenged by Thomas J. Talley. Responding directly to the claims of pagan influence, Talley writes:

---

6. Frank Williams, *The Panarion of Epiphanius of Salamis: Books II and III* (Leiden: Brill, 1994), 51-52.

7. Larsen, *The Oxford Handbook of Christmas*, 5.

> There is no such calendar, nor is there any meaningful basis for the associate of the Julian date, January 6, with any festival connected with the winter solstice in the twentieth-century before Christ. Festivals may have existed in Egyptian antiquity, but they could not for long be associated with any fixed date in that wandering calendar.[8]

"Talley continues,

> "When all is said and done, from all of the evidence we have considered for a pagan background to Epiphany, nothing points definitely to a widespread festival on January 6... Egyptian data will show that the feast of the Epiphany at Alexandria was focused on Christ's baptism..."[9]

While the History of Religions hypothesis dominated early scholarship, a growing number of historians and theologians began to challenge its assumptions. They argued that the date of December 25 was not borrowed from paganism at all, but rather born out of Christian theological reflection. This alternative view—known as the *Calculation* or *Computation Hypothesis*—suggests that early believers arrived at December 25 through sacred reasoning rather than cultural imitation. Instead of asking, *"What pagan festival did Christians*

---

8. Thomas J. Talley, *The Origins of the Liturgical Year: Second, Emended Edition* (New York, NY: Pueblo Publishing, 1991), 111.

9. Talley, *The Origins of the Liturgical Year*, 111.

copy?" this hypothesis asks, *"What did early Christians believe about the life and timing of the Messiah that led them to this date?"* As we'll see in the following chapters, the so-called "copycat" claims will be addressed head-on and shown to rest on assumptions foreign to both Scripture and early Christian thought.

Before exploring how early Christians calculated December 25, it helps to understand two key points on the ancient calendar: the *winter solstice* and the *vernal equinox*. The winter solstice, around December 21, marks the shortest day and longest night of the year—the turning point when the sun begins its return and the days grow longer. The vernal equinox, around March 21, marks the beginning of spring, when day and night are equal in length. Ancient peoples viewed these as symbols of rebirth and renewal. These seasonal markers later became significant in Christian thought because the dates associated with Jesus's conception, crucifixion, and birth were closely tied to them.

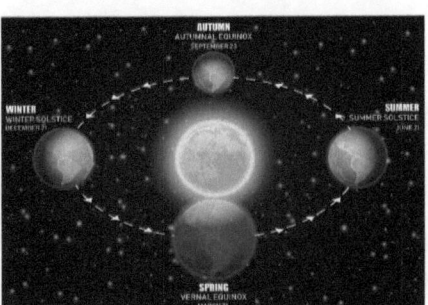

The relationship between the earth's position and the solstices and equinoxes. (Image licensed for use by the author)

The *Computation Hypothesis* was developed by French scholar Louis Duchesne in the late nineteenth century, emerging around the same time as Hermann Usener's work.[10] In essence, many early Christians believed that Jesus's conception—or incarnation—occurred on the same date as His crucifixion, and thus His birth would fall nine months later. This idea stems from an ancient Jewish belief that prophets or great figures lived "integral" years—dying on the same date as either their birth or conception. According to this reasoning, if Jesus died on March 25 (the spring equinox in the Roman calendar), then He was conceived on that same date and born nine months later, on December 25. The Eastern Church, following a similar calculation, placed the crucifixion on April 6, resulting in a birth date of January 6 for the feast of Epiphany.

In the Jewish context, the Passover was not viewed as a single, isolated event. When the Jews were exiled to Babylon in 586 B.C. , Aramaic—not Hebrew—became the common language for many who no longer understood biblical Hebrew. To help them engage with Scripture, *Targumim* were developed. A *Targum* (plural: *Targumim*) is an ancient Jewish Aramaic translation, paraphrase, or interpretive rendering of the Hebrew Scriptures. One of these texts, the *Palestinian Targum on Exodus*, contains a section known as the "Poem of the Four Nights," which connects four key events to the Passover: the creation of the world, the binding of Isaac, the deliverance from Egypt, and the coming of the Messiah.[11]

Furthermore, the earliest textual evidence linking Passover to the redemptive work of Christ appears in a second-century document known as the *Epistula Apostolorum* (*Epistle to the Apostles*). Originally

---

10. Louis Duchesne, *Origines du culte chrétien* [*Origins of Christian Worship*] (Paris: Thorin, 1889), cited in Paul F. Bradshaw, ed., *The Oxford Handbook of Christian Worship* (Oxford: Oxford University Press, 2015), 34.

11. Talley, *The Origins of the Liturgical Year*, 3.

written in Greek and preserved only in Ethiopic, this apocryphal epistle affirms that "Passover was surely kept in the night from 14 to 15 Nisan, [as] the memorial of the death of Jesus."

Talley notes that for early Christians, the celebration of the Passion was not a detached commemoration of Jesus' suffering but the remembrance of the entire redemptive mystery—His incarnation, passion, resurrection, and glorification—focused on the cross as the locus of divine triumph.[12]

This provides compelling evidence that the expectation of the incarnation has always been deeply connected to the Christian understanding of Passover. In *Tractate Rosh Hashanah*—a section of the Babylonian Talmud outlining the laws of the Jewish New Year and the ancient process for determining the months based on the new moon—a fascinating dispute is recorded between Rabbi Eliezer and Rabbi Joshua. Rabbi Joshua argues that the following events occurred in the month of Nisan: the creation of the world, the birth of the patriarchs, the visitation of Rachel and Hannah, Joseph's release from prison, the end of Israel's bondage in Egypt, and their ultimate redemption "in time to come."[13]

I have identified at least ten ancient sources that affirm the credibility and theological coherence of the *Computation Hypothesis*. Collectively, these sources demonstrate that early Christians did not celebrate the birth of Christ on December 25 because of pagan influence, but out of a sincere conviction that the incarnation itself occurred on that date. For them, the timing of Christ's birth was not borrowed from surrounding cultures but derived from prophetic expectation and theological reflection rooted in Scripture.

---

12. Ibid, 6.

13. Babylonian Talmud, Rosh Hashanah 10b–11a.

Tertullian of Carthage: Adversus Judaeos [Against The Jews] (c.200 A.D.)

Tertullian of Carthage was the most prolific Christian author to write in Latin before the fourth century, producing an extensive body of theological and apologetic literature.[14] His influence earned him the title *"Father of Latin Theology."*[15] He was among the first Christian writers to distinguish between the Old and New Testaments, to affirm the authority of all four Gospels, and to acknowledge that they were written either by the apostles themselves or by their close associates.[16] In his treatise *Against Praxeas*, Tertullian employed the terminology *tres personae* ("three persons") and *una substantia* ("one substance"), language that later became the standard Latin formulation for expressing the doctrine of the Trinity.[17]

In *Adversus Judaeos* (*Against the Jews*), chapter 8—written around A.D. 200—Tertullian records that the 14th of Nisan (the day of the crucifixion according to the Gospel of John) in the year Jesus died corresponded to March 25 in the Roman solar calendar. March 25, of course, falls nine months before December 25 and was later recognized

---

14. Everett Ferguson, *Church History, Volume One: From Christ to the Pre-Reformation: The Rise and Growth of the Church in Its Cultural, Intellectual, and Political Context*, 2nd ed. (Grand Rapids, MI: Zondervan, 2013), 126-127.

15. Alec Gilmore, https://ref.ly/logosres/cncsdctntrprttn?ref=Page.p+190&off=3126&ctx=+of+Latin+theology%2c+~one+of+the+first+to+ in *A Concise Dictionary of Bible Origins and Interpretation* (London; New York: T&T Clark, 2006), 190–191.

16. Gilmore, "Tertullian," 190–191.

17. Ferguson, *Church History, Vol One*, 126-127.

DEBUNKING THE PAGAN ROOTS OF CHRISTMAS

by the Church as the Feast of the Annunciation—the commemoration of the conception of Jesus. Tertullian writes:

> And the suffering of this "extermination" was perfected within the times of the lxx hebdomads [70 weeks *Hebdomads* is Latin for *"weeks"*] , under Tiberius Cæsar, in the consulate of Rubellius Geminus and Fufius Geminus, in the month of March, at the times of the Passover, on the eighth day before the calends of April, on the first day of unleavened bread, on which they slew the lamb at even, just as had been enjoined by Moses. Accordingly, all the synagogue of Israel did slay Him, saying to Pilate, when he was desirous to dismiss Him, "His blood be upon us, and upon our children;[18]

For clarity, the term *calends* refers to the first day of the month. The Romans counted backward from three fixed points in each month: the *Calends*, the *Nones*, and the *Ides*. The first day of the month was called the *Calends*—from which the modern word *calendar* is derived. The *Nones* usually fell on the fifth (or occasionally the seventh) day, and the *Ides* on the thirteenth (or sometimes the fifteenth).[19]

Therefore, Tertullian's reference to *"the eighth day before the calends of April"* corresponds to March 25. Using the Gospel of John

---

18. Tertullian, *Adversus Judaeos* [*Against the Jews*], in *Ante-Nicene Fathers*, vol. 3, ed. Alexander Roberts and James Donaldson (Buffalo, NY: Christian Literature Publishing Co., 1885), ch. 8.

19. Walter A. Elwell and Barry J. Beitzel, "Calendars, Ancient and Modern," in *Baker Encyclopedia of the Bible* (Grand Rapids, MI: Baker Book House, 1988), 401.

as his chronological source, Tertullian concluded that Jesus died on March 25. This apologetic treatise, composed around A.D. 200 and drawing extensively from the Hebrew prophets to identify Jesus of Nazareth as the promised Messiah[20], contains the earliest known reference linking March 25—the date of the crucifixion—with December 25—the date of His birth.

Hippolytus Of Rome (c. 235 A.D.)

Our second source comes from Hippolytus of Rome, a prominent third-century writer and theologian who emerged as a significant figure in the early Christian church. He came to Rome from the Eastern Mediterranean, possibly Egypt, and was the last major ecclesiastical writer in Greek at Rome.[21] Hippolytus authored several works in the early third century which provide valuable insight to our discussion:

Commentary on Daniel 4.23.3

Hippolytus' Commentary on Daniel is a significant early Christian exegetical work with several notable characteristics. It is the earliest surviving orthodox commentary on Daniel.[22] Yale University scholar T.C. Schmidt dates this work between 202—211, a time of great per-

---

20. John M'Clintock and James Strong, "Tertullian(us), Quintus Septimius Florens," in *Cyclopædia of Biblical, Theological, and Ecclesiastical Literature* (New York: Harper & Brothers, Publishers, 1881), 289.

21. Ferguson, E. "Hippolytus (c. 170–c. 236)." In *New Dictionary of Theology: Historical and Systematic*, edited by Martin Davie, Tim Grass, Stephen R. Holmes, John McDowell, and T. A. Noble, 410–11.

22. E. Ferguson, "Hippolytus (c. 170–c. 236)", 410.

DEBUNKING THE PAGAN ROOTS OF CHRISTMAS 41

secution for Christians in the Roman Empire.[23] In his commentary Hippolytus states:

> For the first advent of our Lord in the flesh, when he was born in Bethlehem, was December 25th, a Wednesday, while Augustus was in his forty-second year, but from Adam, five thousand and five hundred years. He suffered in the thirty-third year, March 25th, Friday, the eighteenth year of Tiberius Caesar, while Rufus and Roubellion were Consuls.[24]

Hippolytus wrote this commentary to comfort his fellow Christians who were suffering for their faith. This suffering was not feared, but gladly embraced. He suffered martyrdom himself in 235 AD after being exiled to Sardinia.[25] Schmidt concludes that according to this passage, Jesus was born on December 25th, the Winter Solstice, and died on the Passover, Friday, March 25th 29 AD, the Vernal Equinox.[26] Admittedly, there are some who doubt the validity of this passage because the manuscript evidence for it is contradictory. There are six Greek manuscripts and a medieval Slavonic translation which contain the passage at hand. Five of the seven contain the date of December 25. This has led some scholars to believe the commentary was edited by a later scribe and that Hippolytus did not record it himself. This

---

23. T. C. Schmidt, "Introduction," in *Hippolytus of Rome: Commentary on Daniel*, trans. T. C. Schmidt (2010), 3.

24. Hippolytus of Rome, *Commentary on Daniel*, trans. T. C. Schmidt (2010), §4.23.

25. Schmidt, "Introduction," in *Commentary on Daniel*, 3.

26. Schmidt, "Appendix 1," in *Commentary on Daniel*, 3.

is of no major consequence because Hippolytus talks about Jesus' birth and the death of Jesus in two other works, his *"Canon"* and his *"Chronicon."* Scholars are united that Hippolytus authored both works.

The Canon of Hippolytus

Around A.D. 222, Hippolytus of Rome composed a work known as *The Canon*, a chronological table designed to calculate key events in salvation history. Unlike his *Commentary on Daniel*, which interprets Scripture verse by verse, *The Canon* is mathematical and theological—an effort to align the story of redemption with a divine timeline. In it, Hippolytus calculated the dates of creation, the incarnation, and the passion of Christ, showing how early Christians viewed time itself as part of God's redemptive plan.

The most notable detail appears in the second row of Cycle 1, which reads: "Genesis of Christ – Wednesday, April 2." This date corresponds to April 2, 2 B.C. The word *genesis* (Greek: γένεσις) means "beginning" or "origin," and scholars debated whether Hippolytus meant Christ's birth or conception. Modern research, especially by T. C. Schmidt, shows that "April 2" in Hippolytus's system aligns with March 25 in the lunar cycle he used.[27] Thus, Hippolytus was referring to Christ's conception—nine months before His birth on December 25.

Taken together, the evidence from *The Canon* provides one of the earliest examples of Christians connecting creation, incarnation, and redemption on a single sacred timeline. For Hippolytus, the story of

---

27. T. C. Schmidt, "Calculating December 25 as the Birth of Jesus," 2010, 547. https://tcschmidt.com/publications

DEBUNKING THE PAGAN ROOTS OF CHRISTMAS

Christ was not anchored in myth or borrowed from pagan festivals, but woven intentionally into the fabric of time itself—a divine pattern that linked the world's creation to its redemption through the person of Jesus.

The Chronicon

Shortly after completing *The Canon*, Hippolytus produced another chronological work known as the *Chronicon*. Whereas *The Canon* focused on the mathematical cycles of the moon and the timing of Passover and Easter, the *Chronicon* presented a broader history of the world—from creation to Christ. In it, Hippolytus continued developing his belief that the key moments of salvation history—from the creation of Adam to the death and resurrection of Jesus—were divinely ordered and prophetically timed. In the *Chronicon*, Hippolytus used Scripture to calculate the number of years from the creation of the world to his own day, around A.D. 235.[28] He writes

> ...from Adam until the transmigration into Babylon under Jeconiah, 57 generations, 4,842 years, 9 months. And after the transmigration into Babylon until the generation of Christ, there was 14 generations, 660 years, and from the generation of Christ until the Passion there was 30 years and from the Passion up until this year which is year 13 of the Emperor Alexander, there is 206 years. Therefore all the years

---

28. T. C. Schmidt, "Calculating December 25 as the Birth of Jesus," 2010, 552. https://tcschmidt.com/publications

from Adam up until year 13 of the Emperor Alexander make 5,738 years.[29]

This passage aligns perfectly with *The Canon*. It states that Jesus died 206 years before the thirteenth year of Emperor Alexander Severus (A.D. 235), placing the crucifixion around A.D. 29—precisely the same date found in both *The Canon* and the *Commentary on Daniel*.[30]

Taken together, Hippolytus's writings reveal that early Christian thinkers were not borrowing from pagan festivals but building a consistent theological and chronological framework rooted in Scripture. For Hippolytus, the timeline of redemption was no accident—it was intentional, mathematical, and prophetic.

As we turn to Clement of Alexandria, we find this same impulse expressed not through calendars and chronology but through philosophy and theology. Writing several decades earlier, Clement approached the mystery of Christ's coming from a different angle, showing that divine wisdom and timing were woven into both revelation and reason.

Clement of Alexandria (c.198-203 A.D.)

Clement of Alexandria was a Christian philosopher who succeeded his teacher Pantaenus as head of the famous Catechetical School of Alexandria around A.D. 180. Alexandria was home to the largest

---

29. Hippolytus of Rome, *Chronicon* §§686–688 (A.D. 235), trans. T. C. Schmidt in "Calculating December 25 as the Birth of Jesus," 2010, 8, https://tcschmidt.com/publications.

30. Schmidt, *"Calculating December 25 as the Birth of Jesus,"* 553.

DEBUNKING THE PAGAN ROOTS OF CHRISTMAS

Jewish community in the Greco-Roman world. As leader of this influential center of learning—a hub of Gnostic, pagan, and Jewish thought—Clement was uniquely positioned to defend the Christian faith through rational argumentation that would resonate with the intellectual climate of his day.

Clement authored several works presenting Christianity as the true philosophy that leads to the ideal form of life. His three most significant surviving works are the *Protrepticus* (*Exhortation to the Greeks*), *Paedagogus* (*The Instructor*), and *Stromateis* (*Miscellanies* or *Patchwork*).[31] The *Stromata* is a wide-ranging composition that weaves together Scripture, philosophy, and history. Clement draws from both Greek and non-Greek sources, using whatever insights he finds profitable, while refuting heresies and exploring diverse branches of knowledge. The eclectic nature of his writing justifies the title *Stromata*, meaning "Miscellanies" or "Patchwork."[32] In the *Stromata* 1.21.145-146, Clement writes

> From the birth of Christ, therefore, to the death of Commodus are, in all, 194 years, 1 month, 13 days. And there are those who have determined not only the year of our Savior's genesis, but even the day, which they say took place in the twenty-eighth year of Augustus on the 25th of Pachon... And treating of his

---

31. Jordon H. Edwards, "Clement of Alexandria," in *The Essential Lexham Dictionary of Church History*, ed. Michael A. G. Haykin (Bellingham, WA: Lexham Press, 2022).

32. Eusebius of Caesaria, "The Church History of Eusebius," in *Eusebius: Church History, Life of Constantine the Great, and Oration in Praise of Constantine*, ed. Philip Schaff and Henry Wace, trans. Arthur Cushman McGiffert, vol. 1, A Select Library of the Nicene and Post-Nicene Fathers of the Christian Church, Second Series (New York: Christian Literature Company, 1890), 260.

> passion, with very great accuracy, some say that it took place in the sixteenth year of Tiberius, on the 25th of Phamenoth, but others the 25th of Pharmuthi and others say that on the 19th of Pharmuthi the Savior suffered. Indeed, others say that he came to be on the 24th or 25th of Pharmuthi."[33]

Clement is using the Egyptian calendar, which was a mobile solar calendar, but his calculations regarding the conception, birth, and death of Jesus reflect the same pattern observed in Hippolytus. He states that Jesus was born 194 years, one month, and thirteen days before the death of Emperor Commodus—a timeline which, according to Schmidt, would correspond to January 6.[34] He places the *genesis* (or conception) of Jesus on the 25th of Pachon or the 24th/25th of Pharmuthi (approximately March 20–21), coinciding with the Vernal Equinox in the Egyptian calendar.[35]

Finally, Clement dates the death of Jesus to the 25th of Phamenoth or the 19th/25th of Pharmuthi. From this, one can conclude that Clement used the same method of correlating Jesus' conception, birth, and death that we find in Hippolytus. Both hold that Jesus was conceived and crucified at the time of the Passover and Vernal Equinox, affirming an early Christian tradition that viewed these events as divinely synchronized in salvation history.

---

33. Clement of Alexandria, *The Stromata, or Miscellanies*, 1.21.145–146, in *The Ante-Nicene Fathers*, vol. 2, ed. Alexander Roberts and James Donaldson (Buffalo, NY: Christian Literature Publishing Co., 1885), 338.

34. Schmidt, *"Calculating December 25 as the Birth of Jesus,"* 562.

35. Ibid, 562.

DEBUNKING THE PAGAN ROOTS OF CHRISTMAS

Clement's calculations mark one of the earliest efforts to align the dates of Jesus' conception, birth, and death as divinely ordered events. His approach set the stage for later Christian chronologists, such as Julius Africanus, who would build upon this same tradition in tracing God's redemptive timeline through history.

Julius Africanus (221 A.D.)

Julius Africanus, often regarded as the father of Christian chronology, lived during the late second and early third centuries and was a near contemporary of Clement. Apparently of Palestinian origin rather than African, he was converted to Christianity after a long period of military service and extensive travel.[36] Africanus sought to construct a universal history that traced God's redemptive plan from creation to Christ.

His work, the *Chronographiai*, or more commonly in English, *Chronography or Chronicle*, survives only in fragments, but it played a pivotal role in shaping early Christian thought about sacred time. Like Clement and Hippolytus, Africanus attempted to harmonize biblical events with historical and astronomical data, reflecting the conviction that the incarnation was not random but occurred at a precise, providentially appointed moment in history.

In Fragment 1 (c. A.D. 221), Africanus explains that:

> "For the Jews, deriving their origin from them as descendants of Abraham, having been taught a modest

---

36. Justo Luis González, "Sextus Julius Africanus (?–ca. 245)," in *The Westminster Dictionary of Theologians*, ed. Justo L. González, trans. Suzanne E. Hoeferkamp Segovia (Louisville, KY; London: Westminster John Knox Press, 2006), 309.

mind, and one such as becomes men, together with the truth by the spirit of Moses, have handed down to us, by their extant Hebrew histories, the number of 5500 years as the period up to the advent of the Word of salvation, that was announced to the world in the time of the sway of the Caesars."[37]

Elsewhere, in another surviving fragment preserved by George Syncellus, he adds:

For the first advent of our Lord in the flesh, when He was born in Bethlehem, took place eight days before the Kalends of January, on the fourth day [of the week], while Augustus was in his forty-second year, and from Adam five thousand and five hundred years. He suffered in the thirty-third year, eight days before the Kalends of April, on the day of Preparation, the fifteenth year of Tiberius Caesar."[38]

Africanus' writings demonstrate that early Christian chronology was rooted in the conviction that Christ entered history at the divinely appointed completion of 5,500 years from creation. His calculation places both the birth and death of Christ within this frame-

---

37. Julius Africanus, *Fragment 1* (A.D. 221), in *The Ante-Nicene Fathers*, vol. 6, ed. Alexander Roberts and James Donaldson (Buffalo, NY: Christian Literature Publishing Co., 1886), 130.

38. Julius Africanus, fragment from Chronographiai, cited in George Syncellus, Chronographia 390, trans. in The Ante-Nicene Fathers, vol. 6, ed. Alexander Roberts and James Donaldson (Buffalo, NY: Christian Literature Publishing Co., 1886), 130.

work—born on December 25 (eight days before the Kalends of January) and crucified on March 25 (eight days before the Kalends of April). Both dates correspond to the Vernal Equinox and reflect the belief that the incarnation and the passion occurred at the same cosmic moment when light conquers darkness. Africanus, therefore, stands as a key witness to the Christian understanding that the timing of Christ's coming was the fulfillment of prophetic chronology, not a borrowing from pagan festivals.

Augustine of Hippo and the Donatists (4th-5th Century)

Augustine of Hippo was born at Thagaste, North Africa (modern-day Algeria), to a pagan father, Patricius, a member of the town council, and his Christian mother, Monica, through whom he was made a *catechumen*—a Christian convert under instruction before baptism—in infancy.[39] After years of philosophical searching and worldly ambition, Augustine converted to Christianity while serving as a professor in Rome and became one of the Church's greatest defenders of the faith. He would go on to write twenty-two volumes in twelve years, including *The City of God*, a monumental work in which human history is interpreted as a struggle between the earthly city, founded on self-love, and the City of God, founded on divine grace.[40]

Pastor, author, and urban apologist Jerome Gay writes,

---

39. F. L. Cross and Elizabeth A. Livingstone, eds., *The Oxford Dictionary of the Christian Church* (Oxford; New York: Oxford University Press, 2005), 129.

40. C. Stephen Evans, *Pocket Dictionary of Apologetics & Philosophy of Religion* (Downers Grove, IL: InterVarsity Press, 2002), 23.

Augustine was a master in rhetoric and to use modern vernacular he had what many in urban communities and fans of hip-hop called "bars"; he's given us quotes like "unity in things necessary, liberty and things doubtful, charity in all things"; with love for mankind and hatred of sin" (this is where we get the phrase "love the sinner, hate the sin" from); "Jesus Christ will be the Lord of all, or he will not be Lord at all," and many others.[41]

In one of his sermons written to guide believers in the proper spiritual celebration of the major feasts of Christmas and Epiphany, Augustine writes:

"With good reason have the heretical Donatists never wished to celebrate this day [Epiphany] with us: they neither love unity, nor are they in communion with the Eastern Church where that star appeared. Let us, however, celebrate the Manifestation of our Lord and Savior Jesus Christ on which He harvested the first fruits of the gentiles, any the unity of the Gentiles."[42]

The Donatists' refusal to celebrate with the Catholics was part of a larger schism that fundamentally questioned where the true

---

41. Jerome Gay, *The Whitewashing of Christianity: A Hidden Past, a Hurtful Present, and a Hopeful Future* (Chicago, IL: 13th & Joan, 2021), 126.

42. Thomas Comerford Lawler, trans., *St. Augustine: Sermons for Christmas and Epiphany. Ancient Christian Writers*, no. 15. (Westminster, Md. 1952), p. 170

Church resided. Augustine argued that the Church was one and Catholic—the body of Christ—and that any divergence from its head or body was, by definition, outside the Church.[43]

Augustine's mention of the star and the visit of the Magi clearly identifies this as a reference to the Feast of the Epiphany. His comment reveals that the Donatists refused to celebrate Epiphany—the feast commemorating the manifestation of Christ to the Gentiles—yet he never accuses them of rejecting Christmas, a silence that speaks volumes. Since the Donatist schism began around A.D. 311, their apparent acceptance of Christmas implies that the Feast of the Nativity was already established in North Africa before the division.[44] Both groups therefore inherited the celebration from a shared earlier tradition. This suggests that the observance of Christ's birth on December 25 predates the Donatist schism and may even have originated in North Africa rather than later in Rome.

Taken together, the testimonies of Tertullian, Hippolytus, Clement of Alexandria, Julius Africanus, and Augustine present a consistent historical pattern: the dating of Christ's birth on December 25 emerged from theological reflection and chronological calculation, not from pagan imitation. Long before the rise of later Roman festivals, these early Christian witnesses—spanning regions from North Africa to Alexandria and Palestine—recognized the incarnation as a divinely ordered event rooted in Scripture and sacred time. By the mid–fourth century, this tradition was no longer theoretical but for-

---

43. Chester D. Hartranft, https://ref.ly/logosres/npnf04?ref=Page.p+383&off=1495&ctx=+Only+Begotten+Son%2c+~and+for+its+body+the in *St. Augustin: The Writings against the Manichaeans and against the Donatists*, ed. Philip Schaff, vol. 4, A Select Library of the Nicene and Post-Nicene Fathers of the Christian Church, First Series (Buffalo, NY: Christian Literature Company, 1887), 383.

44. Talley, *The Origins of the Liturgical Year, 86-87.*

mally recorded in the Roman calendar itself, as seen in the Chronography of 354. What began as a theological conviction among early Christian thinkers was soon woven into the fabric of Roman history itself.

Chronography of 354

The *Chronography of 354*—a title given by the 19th-century historian Theodor Mommsen to an anonymous almanac compiled for Christian use —represents the earliest explicit Roman record of the celebration of Christ's birth on December 25.[45] The work survives as an illuminated codex prepared by the calligrapher Furius Dionysius Filocalus for a Roman nobleman named Valentinus and served as both a civic and ecclesiastical calendar. It includes lists of Roman officials, festivals, consuls, and Christian commemorations, demonstrating the coexistence of imperial and ecclesial observances within mid–fourth-century Rome.

As Thomas J. Talley explains,

> "Our earliest documentary evidence for the observance of the nativity of Christ on December 25th shows it to be such a turning point of the liturgical year. This document is the *Chronography of 354*, an almanac presenting lists of Roman holidays, councils, city prefects, and two lists of burial dates—one of Roman bishops and another of martyrs, with the indication of the cemeteries in each case. Both of these burial lists are in calendrical order, not historical or-

---

45. Cross and Livingstone, *The Oxford Dictionary of the Christian Church*, 343

der, and the first date given in the *Depositio Martyrum* is December 25."⁴⁶

Among its entries appears the now-famous notation:

"VIII kal. Jan. natus Christus in Betleem Iudeae"—translated, *"Eight days before the Kalends of January, Christ was born in Bethlehem of Judea."

The significance of this development can hardly be overstated. In a city once defined by its pantheon of gods and imperial cult, Rome—the very heart of paganism—had reoriented its sacred calendar around the birth of a Jewish man who claimed to be God. As Talley notes, the *Chronography of 354* reveals that both the *Depositio Martyrum* and the Roman calendar itself began on December 25, marking the Nativity of Christ as the starting point of the liturgical year.⁴⁷

The term Depositio Martyrum *[Burial or The Laying to Rest of the Martyrs]* refers to an early Roman catalog listing the burial dates of Christian martyrs. Its placement beginning on December 25 highlights that the cycle of Christian remembrance and worship itself was anchored to the birth of Christ.

This means that by A.D. 336, the rhythm of Christian worship in Rome no longer revolved around the solar festivals of the empire but around the Son of Righteousness who had entered history. The irony is profound: the empire that once demanded divine honors for its

---

46. Talley, *The Origins of the Liturgical Year*, 85.

47. Ibid, 85.

rulers now measured its sacred time by the birth of a crucified Messiah. What began as the faith of an oppressed and persecuted minority had, within a few centuries, transformed the very structure of Roman time itself.

By this point, the evidence is undeniable. From North Africa to Rome, the celebration of Christ's birth on December 25 had already taken root long before any supposed pagan influence. What follows are a few final witnesses—brief but significant voices like the anonymous author of *On Solstices and Equinoxes*, Gregory of Nazianzus, John Chrysostom, and Augustine in *On the Trinity*—each echoing the same conviction. Their testimonies serve not to introduce a new argument, but to confirm the one already made: that the dating of Christmas arose from Christian belief, not pagan borrowing.

On Solstices and Equinoxes... (4th Century)

An anonymous 4th-century Christian treatise titled "*On Solstices and Equinoxes* of the Conception and Nativity of Our Lord Jesus Christ and of John the Baptist" preserves the same theological reasoning we saw in Hippolytus and Africanus. It states,

> Our Lord was conceived on the 25th of March; it is the day of the Passover and of the Lord's suffering as well as his conception. He suffered on the very same day that he was conceived.[48]

---

48. Anonymous, On the Solstices and the Equinoxes of the Conception and Nativity of Our Lord Jesus Christ and of John the Baptist, trans. Isabella Image, ed. Roger Pearse (2022), 4. https://www.roger-pearse.com/weblog/2022/02/05/de-solstitiis-et-aequinoctiis-cpl-2277-now-online-in-english/

This early text affirms the belief that Christ's conception and crucifixion occurred on the same date—the spring equinox—and that His birth, nine months later, fell on December 25. The treatise shows that this calculation was widely accepted among Christians long before later critics claimed pagan influence.

St. Gregory of Nazianzus (c. 380 A.D.)

Writing in the late 4th century, Gregory of Nazianzus—known as "The Theologian"[49] —preached that the Christian celebration of Christ's birth was distinct from any pagan festival. In *Oration 38* he calls it both the "Theophany" and the "Birthday," proclaiming,

> (3) For the present Festival is the Theophany or Birth-day [Nativity], for it is called both, two titles being given to the one thing. For God was manifested to man by birth...The name Theophany is given to it in reference to the Manifestation, and that of Birthday in respect of His Birth.

> (4) This is our present Festival; it is this which we are celebrating today, the Coming of God to Man...Therefore let us keep the Feast, not after the manner of a heathen festival, but after a godly sort; not after the way of the world, but in a fashion above the

---

49. F. L. Cross and Elizabeth A. Livingstone, eds., *The Oxford Dictionary of the Christian Church* (Oxford; New York: Oxford University Press, 2005), 715.

world; not as our own but as belonging to Him Who is ours, or rather as our Master's; not as of weakness, but as of healing; not as of creation, but of re-creation.⁵⁰

Gregory's sermon demonstrates that by this time the Feast of the Nativity was firmly established and explicitly distinguished from pagan customs, celebrated as the holy moment when "God was manifested to man by birth."

John Chrysostom (386 A.D.)

Half a century after the *Chronography of 354*, John Chrysostom, bishop of Antioch, preached a homily on December 20, A.D. 386, anticipating the Feast of the Nativity five days later on December 25. In another sermon (*Homily VI on St. Philogonius*), he writes:

> "A feast day is about to arrive and it is the most holy, august, and awesome of all feasts; it would be no mistake to call it the chief and mother of all holy days. What feast is that? The day of Christ's birth in the flesh. It is from this day that the feasts of the Theophany, the sacred Pasch[a], the Ascension, and Pentecost had their source and foundation. Had Christ not been born in the flesh, he would not have been baptized, which is the Theophany or Manifestation; nor

---

50. Gregory of Nazianzus, *Oration 38: On the Theophany, or On the Nativity of Christ* 3–4, in *Nicene and Post-Nicene Fathers*, Second Series, vol. 7, ed. Philip Schaff and Henry Wace (New York: Christian Literature Publishing Co., 1894), accessed November 3, 2025, https://www.newadvent.org/fathers/310238.htm.

DEBUNKING THE PAGAN ROOTS OF CHRISTMAS

would he have been crucified, which is the Pasch[a]; nor would he have sent down the Spirit, which is Pentecost. So, it is that, just as different rivers arise from a source, these other feasts have their beginnings from the birth of Christ."[51]

Chrysostom's words confirm that the December 25 celebration was already established in Antioch and that he viewed it as the source and foundation of all other Christian feasts.

Augustine of Hippo, *On the Trinity* (c. 399–426 A.D.)

In his later work *On the Trinity*, Augustine echoes the same ancient chronology:

For He is believed to have been conceived on the 25th of March, upon which day also He suffered; so the womb of the Virgin, in which He was conceived, where no one of mortals was begotten, corresponds to the new grave in which He was buried, wherein was never man laid, neither before nor since. But He

---

51. "A Homily in Preparation for the Celebration of Christmas According to Saint John Chrysostom," *Orthodox Ethos*, accessed November 16, 2025, https://www.orthodoxethos.com/post/a-homily-in-preparation-for-the-celebration-of-christmas-according-to-saint-john-chrysostom

was born, according to tradition, upon December the 25th.[52]

Writing more than a century after Hippolytus, Augustine confirms that the March 25 conception and December 25 birth were still the standard Christian understanding. His statement demonstrates continuity—an unbroken line of belief that the timing of Christ's incarnation and passion was divinely ordered, not culturally borrowed.

Chapter Conclusion

From Tertullian's defense of Christian distinctiveness to Augustine's final reflections on the divine symmetry of Christ's conception and birth, the evidence speaks with one voice. Long before Christianity held cultural power, believers across the ancient world—from North Africa to Alexandria, from Palestine to Rome—affirmed December 25 not as a borrowed pagan date but as the culmination of sacred time. Hippolytus, Clement, Africanus, and Augustine each tied the incarnation to the providential rhythm of creation and redemption; the *Chronography of 354* simply recorded what was already the lived conviction of the early Church. Later witnesses like the anonymous author of *On Solstices and Equinoxes*, Gregory of Nazianzus, John Chrysostom, and Augustine in *On the Trinity* confirmed that conviction for generations to come. The celebration of Christ's birth was never about mimicking paganism—it was about marking the moment

---

52. Augustine, *On the Trinity* 4.5.9, in *Nicene and Post-Nicene Fathers*, First Series, vol. 3, ed. Philip Schaff (Buffalo, NY: Christian Literature Publishing Co., 1887), accessed November 3, 2025, https://www.newadvent.org/fathers/130104.htm.

heaven touched earth, when eternity stepped into time and transformed even the Roman calendar into a testimony of grace.

4

SATURNALIA & SOL INVICTUS

THEY NOT LIKE US

In his viral track "They Not Like Us," Kendrick Lamar calls out the hypocrisy of cultural appropriation — when someone imitates a culture they don't belong to for personal gain. Lamar's frustration wasn't just artistic rivalry; it was about authenticity. He was saying, "you can copy the sound, but you can't copy the soul. You can borrow the look, but not the lived experience."

That's exactly what we're dealing with when people claim that Christmas was "copied" from pagan festivals like Saturnalia or Sol Invictus. The accusation assumes imitation — that early Christians borrowed from Roman culture to invent a holiday. But just like Kendrick's message, the truth is simple: They not like us.

The celebration of Christmas wasn't about cultural mimicry; it was about divine manifestation. Where Saturnalia honored Saturn, a fading god of harvest, and Sol Invictus praised a man-made "unconquered sun," the Christian feast of Christmas celebrates the Son who conquered sin and death. The difference isn't just theological — it's historical.

The evidence shows that the dates, rituals, and meanings of Saturnalia and Sol Invictus were fundamentally different from Christmas.

DEBUNKING THE PAGAN ROOTS OF CHRISTMAS   61

What connected the early Church wasn't a borrowed festival — it was the Incarnation, the belief that God Himself stepped into history. The Roman festivals were about indulgence and inversion; Christmas is about incarnation and redemption.

In this chapter, we'll look closely at the primary sources — writers like Lucian, Macrobius, and Tertullian — to see what Saturnalia really was, how long it lasted, what it celebrated, and why early Christians didn't join in. We'll also explore how Sol Invictus, a political invention of Emperor Aurelian, came centuries later — after Christians were already commemorating December 25th as the birth of Christ. Because when you line up the evidence side by side, one thing becomes undeniable: they not like us.

Rome & Christian Persecution

Before we even talk about Saturnalia or Sol Invictus, we need to deal with one glaring historical reality: Christians weren't copying Roman festivals — they were being killed for rejecting them.

If Christians had been blending their worship with Rome's gods, Rome wouldn't have persecuted them. The Roman Empire wasn't offended by another god; it was offended by the only God. The earliest believers didn't just refuse to participate in pagan feasts — they refused to even sprinkle a pinch of incense before the emperor's image. And for that refusal, many were tortured, imprisoned, or executed. From the late 2nd century through the early 4th, persecution came in waves, each wave proving just how unwilling Christians were to compromise.

The Rise of Sol Invictus and Syncretism under Septimius Severus (193–211 A.D.)

When Septimius Severus rose to power, the Roman Empire was recovering from years of civil war and instability. Although he had restored order, Rome was still surrounded by barbarian threats and plagued by internal unrest. To unify the empire, Severus pursued a policy of religious syncretism—a blending of beliefs he hoped would create social harmony and prevent further division.[1]

He proposed a plan to unite all Roman subjects under the worship of Sol Invictus, "the Unconquered Sun," allowing everyone to honor their local gods as long as they acknowledged the Sun as supreme. This politically motivated religion was meant to hold the empire together, but it clashed directly with two faiths that refused to compromise—Judaism and Christianity.[2]

Both groups rejected the notion that all gods were equal and refused to acknowledge any deity above the one true God. In response, Severus outlawed conversion to Judaism or Christianity under penalty of death.[3] His effort to create harmony through compromise became the catalyst for new waves of persecution.

It was during this time that Perpetua and Felicity [English form of the original Latin "Felicitas"], two North African women—one a noblewoman, the other her servant—were executed in Carthage for refusing to renounce Christ. Perpetua is the heroine of the *"Martyrdom of Saints Perpetua and Felicitas."* Her companions were the slaves Felicitas and Revocatus, and two other young women, Saturninus and Secundulus. When arrested, Perpetua's father tried to persuade her to save her life by abandoning her faith. She answered that, just as

---

1. Justo L. Gonzalez, *The Story of Christianity Volume 1: The Early Church to the Dawn of the Reformation*, 2nd ed. (New York, NY: HarperCollins, 2010), 97-98.

2. Gonzalez, *The Story of Christianity Volume 1*, 97-98.

3. Ibid, 97-98.

everything has a meaning and it is useless to try to give it a different name she had the name of Christian, and this could not be changed.[4]

Felicitas was eight months pregnant when arrested. It was unlawful for pregnant women to be executed, so in an unbelievable testament of courage, she and her comrades prayed that she would give birth prematurely so that she would not be martyred separately from her fellow Christians. Two days before the scheduled execution, she gave birth to a girl and gave her to a fellow Christian woman and prepared for her martyrdom.

One of the assistants to the prison guards said to her: "You suffer so much now, what will you do when you are tossed to the beasts? Little did you think of them when you refused to sacrifice [to the Roman gods]." 'What I am suffering now,' she replied, 'I suffer by myself. But then another will be inside me who will suffer for me, just as I shall be suffering for him." [5]

Perpetua and Felicitas were stripped naked, placed in nets and brought to the arena. The crowd was horrified seeing that Felicitas' breasts were still dripping with milk from having recently given birth. After being dressed in unbelted tunics, they were thrown to a mad heifer (cow). When the heifer tossed Perpetua on her back, she asked for a pin to tie her hair, for loose hair was a sign of mourning, and this was a joyful day for her. The two bleeding women stood in the middle of the arena, bid each other farewell with the kiss of peace, and died by the sword.[6] These two women are a true testament to the phrase

---

4. Herbert Anthony Musurillo, *The Acts of the Christian Martyrs* (London, England: Oxford University Press, 1972), 109.

5. Musurillo, *The Acts of the Christian Martyrs*, 123-124.

6. Ibid, 131.

"black girls rock" and an example of how God has consistently used women throughout history.[7]

Their story remains a defining moment in early Christian witness, illustrating that the Church did not imitate Roman religion; it resisted it, even unto death. So when skeptics claim that Christians borrowed Roman festivals or named their celebrations after pagan gods, history tells a different story. These believers weren't mimicking the empire—they were martyred by it. *They not like us.*

The Decian Persecution (249—251 A.D.) — Make Rome Great Again

Fast-forward a few decades. By the time of Emperor Decius, Rome was celebrating its thousandth anniversary (A.D. 247) with grand festivities to the gods. Christians once again refused to join. When plague struck afterward, Romans blamed them for angering the deities.[8] Decius responded with an empire-wide persecution designed to "Make Rome Great Again" by forcing everyone — including Christians — to offer sacrifices to the gods.[9]

This was a reversal of strategy. Decius figured forcing Christians to become apostates and publicly denying their faith was more effective than martyring them, which only seemed to cause Christianity to grow. Tertullian declared:

---

7. Gay Jr, *The Whitewashing of Christianity*, 116.

8. Timothy Paul Jones, *Christian History Made Easy* (Torrance, CA: Rose Publishing, 2017), 34-35.

9. Gonzalez, *The Story of Christianity Volume 1*, 100-101.

> But do your worst, and rack your inventions for tortures for Christians—it is all to no purpose; you do but attract the world, and make it fall the more in love with our religion; the more you mow us down, the thicker we rise; the Christian blood you spill is like the seed you sow, it springs from the earth again, and fructifies the more.[10]

Christians who refused to sacrifice to the Romans gods were imprisoned, tortured, or killed. Even possession of the Scriptures became dangerous. To survive, some believers purchased fake sacrifice certificates; others fled; others died as martyrs. If Christians had been blending their faith with Roman religious customs, Decius' campaign wouldn't have been necessary.

Diocletian & The Great Persecution (303-311 A.D.)

Later, Emperors Diocletian and Galerius unleashed the fiercest persecution yet. Churches were destroyed, Scriptures burned, and Christian leaders thrown into prison. Eusebius records imperial decrees commanding that *"churches be leveled to the ground and the Scriptures be destroyed by fire."*[11]

---

10. Tertullian, *The Apology of Tertullian*, trans. S. Thelwall (London: Society for Promoting Christian Knowledge, 1908), 143.

11. Eusebius, *Church History* 8.4–5, trans. Arthur Cushman McGiffert, in *Nicene and Post-Nicene Fathers*, 2nd ser., vol. 1, ed. Philip Schaff and Henry Wace (Buffalo, NY: Christian Literature Publishing Co., 1890), https://www.newadvent.org/fathers/250108.htm.

Christians were banned from government service, denied civil rights, and commanded to sacrifice to the gods or die. Even as they were hunted, they refused to conform to Roman worship — including festivals like Saturnalia or celebrations of Sol Invictus.

Put Some Respeck On Their Names

From the reign of Septimius Severus in A.D. 193 to Constantine's legalization of Christianity around A.D. 324, believers endured over a century of persecution — *not* because they blended with the empire, but because they refused to bow to it. They were imprisoned, tortured, and killed for rejecting the very festivals and gods that skeptics now claim they supposedly copied. So when people say that Christmas was "borrowed" from pagan Rome, we need to put some "respeck" on the names — and on the history — of the martyrs who paved the way for our faith.

That phrase comes from rapper Birdman's now-iconic 2016 interview on *The Breakfast Club*, where he demanded recognition and respect for his name. In his own way, he was saying, "Don't play with my legacy." The same principle applies here. The men and women of the early church weren't cultural imitators; they were courageous witnesses. They deserve more than casual dismissal through internet memes and half-baked pagan-parallel claims.

To claim that the early Christians adopted Roman holidays is to dishonor the very people who died rather than participate in them. These were believers who refused to sacrifice even a pinch of incense to Caesar, who watched their Scriptures burned, and who went to their deaths singing hymns instead of pledging allegiance to the gods of Rome. Their blood wasn't shed for compromise — it was shed for conviction. And when we repeat myths that say the Church copied the empire, we disrespect that sacrifice.

The truth is simple. The Romans demanded conformity. The Christians chose the cross. They didn't imitate the empire — they were executed by it. So let us put some respeck on their names. They not like us.

Now that we've put some *respeck* on the names of those who suffered for the faith, let's turn to the festivals in question — Saturnalia and Sol Invictus — the celebrations often cited in the claim that Christmas was "copied" from pagan Rome. Because if we're going to have this conversation, we need to deal in facts, not folklore. Before we talk about dates or decorations, we need to ask: *What were these Roman festivals actually about?* What did they celebrate? Who celebrated them? And how do we know?

When we examine the historical sources — writers like Lucian, Macrobius, and even Tertullian himself — we discover that the meaning and practices of Saturnalia were nothing like the Christian celebration of the Incarnation. In fact, the two couldn't be further apart.

Saturnalia – The Original Turnup

If we're going to talk about Saturnalia, let's talk about what it actually was — not what internet memes say it was. Saturnalia was one of Rome's oldest and most popular festivals, dedicated to Saturn, the Roman god of agriculture. It began on December 17 and eventually expanded to a full week of celebrations ending around December 23. [12] The festival marked the end of the planting season and the hope for agricultural abundance in the coming year. Saturnalia's festivities

---

12. Tanya Gulevich, *Encyclopedia of Christmas* (Detroit, MI: Omnigraphics, 2003), 556.

included a general round of gift-giving, merrymaking, and role-reversals so that it became one of the most popular celebrations in the calendar.[13]

According to Macrobius, a fifth-century Roman writer, Saturnalia was originally a rural harvest festival, but by the late Republic and early Empire, it had morphed into a weeklong carnival of excess and social inversion. Masters waited on their slaves, gambling was permitted, and public drunkenness was common.[14] Macrobius makes it clear that Saturnalia was never celebrated on December 25. He writes:

> Our ancestors restricted the Saturnalia to a single day, the fourteenth before the Kalends of January, but, after Gaius Caesar had added two days to December, the day on which the festival was held became the sixteenth before the Kalends of January, with the result that, since the exact day was not commonly known—some observing the addition which Caesar had made to the calendar and others following the old usage —the festival came to be regarded as lasting for more days than one.[15]

Macrobius is clear that Saturnalia was originally a single day event held on December 19 (fourteen days before the Kalends or first of Jan-

---

13. Mark Cartwright, "Temple of Saturn, Roman Forum," *World History Encyclopedia*, last modified April 26, 2012, https://www.worldhistory.org/image/2182/temple-of-saturn-roman-forum/.

14. Macrobius, *The Saturnalia* 1.10.1–23, trans. Percival Vaughan Davies (New York: Columbia University Press, 1969), 70-73.

15. Macrobius, *The Saturnalia, 70*.

uary). Over time, Julius Caesar added two days to December and the original date shifted to December 17 (the sixteenth before the Kalends of January). The confusion over which day to celebrate caused people to celebrate for more than one day. What is clear is that the festival has always been completed prior to December 25.

Lucian of Samosata, a second-century satirist (one who uses humor, irony, exaggeration, etc to expose the flaws of individuals, institutions, or society in general), gives us one of the most colorful accounts. In his dialogue *Saturnalia*, he depicts Saturn himself giving orders for the festival: slaves were to speak freely, everyone could mock their superiors, and even morality took a holiday. Seating arrangements, portions and even service at Roman feasts which typically were arranged according to wealth and social status — were reversed during Saturnalia. The whole point was to turn the world upside down for a week — to indulge, to let loose, and to laugh at the boundaries that normally governed Roman life.

What the Romans now celebrated once a year for a week — was the reality of the Church every day. In Christ, status meant nothing, and love leveled everyone at the foot of the cross. Early Christians didn't just avoid Saturnalia — they condemned it. Tertullian, writing around A.D. 197, rebuked believers who were tempted to join the festivities, saying:

> The Minervalia are as much Minerva's, as the Saturnalia Saturn's; Saturn's, which must necessarily be celebrated even by little slaves at the time of the Saturnalia. New-year's gifts likewise must be caught at, and the Septimontium kept; and all the presents of Midwinter and the feast of Dear Kinsmanship must be exacted; the schools must be wreathed with flowers;

the flamens' wives and the ædiles sacrifice; the school is honoured on the appointed holy-days. The same thing takes place on an idol's birthday; every pomp of the devil is frequented. Who will think that these things are befitting to a Christian master, unless it be he who shall think them suitable likewise to one who is not a master?

Tertullian's frustration shows that some Christians were feeling the cultural pressure to blend in, but the Church's official stance was clear — *don't participate*. In a world where public life revolved around pagan festivals, Christians drew sharp boundaries between the sacred and the secular. They didn't imitate Saturnalia; they resisted it. And that resistance cost them. To celebrate Saturnalia was to acknowledge Saturn — and acknowledging Saturn was idolatry. So when people today say Christmas "came from" Saturnalia, they're essentially saying the very thing that got Christians killed was the thing they secretly adopted. That's not history — that's revisionism.

Saturnalia celebrated a dying god of the harvest; Christmas celebrates the living God made flesh. Saturnalia was about escaping moral order; Christmas is about the divine restoration of it. One exalted human indulgence. The other exalted divine incarnation. You can't confuse the two unless you've never actually looked at either.

So, before we move on to Sol Invictus, it's important to remember: The Roman Saturnalia was never about the "Son" rising — it was about keeping the crops alive. It was fun, it was loud, it was pagan — but it was not prophetic. When Christians proclaimed the birth of Jesus, they weren't echoing Saturnalia's laughter; they were interrupting it with light. They...not...like...us.

The Invincible Son vs. The Unconquered Sun: Debunking The Sol Invictus Myth

Every December, the same tired claim resurfaces — that Christians copied a pagan festival and borrowed Christmas from Rome's celebration of *Sol Invictus*, 'the Unconquered Sun.' It sounds convincing—until you look at the evidence. When the historical record is examined, the claim fades like shadows before sunrise.

Modern critics often say that Christmas was a rebranded sun festival. The assumption is that Emperor Aurelian instituted *Dies Natalis Solis Invicti*—the "Birthday of the Unconquered Sun"—in 274 CE, and that Christians later adopted December 25 to "Christianize" this popular pagan celebration. According to this theory, Christmas would have been the ultimate *diss track*, demonstrating that the "Unconquerable Sun" had indeed been conquered."[16] On the surface, that theory seems logical. After all, both involved light, both used similar language of "birth," and both fell on the same date.

But here's the catch: there's no ancient evidence that Aurelian's festival on December 25 even existed before Christians were already using that date for the birth of Christ. The earliest proof for the *Sol Invictus* festival comes from the Chronography of 354, a Roman calendar compiled 80 years after Aurelian's reign (during the rule of Constantius II). And that's the *same document* that also contains the earliest written reference to December 25 as *Natalis Christi*—the "Birth of Christ." In other words, the earliest evidence we have for

---

16. Walter L. Liefeld, "Luke," in *The Expositor's Bible Commentary: Matthew, Mark, Luke*, ed. Frank E. Gaebelein, vol. 8 (Grand Rapids, MI: Zondervan Publishing House, 1984), 845.

the celebration of Sol Invictus, is the same exact source that dates the birth of Jesus to December 25. Emperor Aurelian (reigned 270–275 CE) did indeed promote the cult of *Sol Invictus*. After defeating the Palmyrene Empire, he credited his victory to the sun god and built a new temple to Sol in Rome around 274 CE. But this was not a long-standing popular festival among the people—it was a state-sponsored cult created for political unity in a fractured empire. Aurelian's aim wasn't to outshine Christianity; it was to consolidate Rome's many eastern and western deities under one imperial sun deity representing the emperor's power. In other words, Aurelian's reign gave prominence to Sol Invictus as an imperial symbol, but there's no proof he tied that devotion to December 25. The evidence of an actual festival comes decades later—after Christmas was already observed in Rome.

As historian Steven Hijmans points out, there is *no ancient record* linking Aurelian's Sol festival to December 25 until decades later, and even then, it's ambiguous. Hijmans concludes:

> The contention that December 25 was an especially popular festival for Sol in late antiquity is equally unfounded, as is the notion that this festival was established by Aurelian when he supposedly instituted a new cult of the sun... it must be stressed, *pace* Usener, that there is no evidence that Aurelian instituted a celebration of Sol on that day. A feast day for Sol on December 25 is not mentioned until eighty years later, in the Calendar of 354 and, subsequently, in 362 by Julian in his Oration to King Helios.

In short, while the winter solstice on or around the 25th of December was well established in the Roman imperial calendar, there is no evidence that a religious celebration of Sol on that day antedated the celebration of Christmas, and none that indicates that Aurelian had a hand in its institution.[17]

So rather than Christianity copying paganism, it may have been the other way around—paganism reacting to Christianity's growing influence and established celebration.

The Chronography of 354 (also known as the Calendar of Philocalus) is our earliest source mentioning both events. On the civil calendar line for December 25 it reads "N INVICTI CM XXX," interpreted as *"Birthday of the Unconquered [Sun]."* Elsewhere in the same document, under the section called the *Depositio Martyrum [Burial of the Martyrs]*, another entry appears for the same day: *"VIII Kal. Ian. natus Christus in Betleem Iudeae"* ("On the eighth day before the Kalends of January [December 25], Christ was born in Bethlehem of Judea").

Two separate entries. Two separate sections. Nothing in the document suggests one was copied from the other. Instead, as Thomas J. Talley notes, the Christian entry marks the beginning of the liturgical year: "From 336, then, we may say that at Rome the nativity of Christ on December 25 marked the beginning of the liturgical year."[18]

---

17. Steven E. Hijmans, *Sol: Image and Meaning of the Sun in Roman Art and Religion, Volume I* (Leiden, Netherlands: Brill, 2024), 588.

18. Talley, *The Origins of the Liturgical Year*, 85.

Talley further notes that the *Depositio Martyrum* ran "from December 25th to December 25th," showing that the date had already become the fixed staring point of the Christian year in Rome.[19] This means the Christian festival was not an imitation of pagan practice—it was a recognized anchor point for Christian worship in Rome.

From the data, several facts emerge clearly:

1. The earliest mention of a December 25 festival for Sol Invictus comes after Christians were already commemorating the Nativity on that date.

2. There is no evidence Aurelian ever instituted that feast day for the Sun.

3. By contrast, Christian sources such as Hippolytus of Rome and others had identified December 25 as the birth of Christ well before Aurelian's reign.

4. Therefore, if any borrowing occurred, it is more plausible that the pagans imitated the Christians, not the other way around.

The assumptions of pagan origins are always trumped by the presentation of evidence. Not a single piece of writing from the fathers of the early church hint at any calendar reforms; they did not believe the date was chosen by the church. They saw the coincidence of the birth of the Son of God and celebration of the pagan sun as a providential sign, as natural proof that God had selected Jesus over the false pagan gods.[20] Dr. Andrew McGowan, Scholar, and President of Berkely Divinity School writes:

---

19. Ibid, 85.

DEBUNKING THE PAGAN ROOTS OF CHRISTMAS 75

It's not until the 12th century that we find the first suggestion that Jesus' birth celebration was deliberately set at the time of pagan feasts. A marginal note on a manuscript of the writings of the Syriac biblical commentator Dionysius bar-Salibi states that in ancient times the Christmas holiday was actually shifted from January 6 to December 25 so that it fell on the same date as the pagan Sol Invictus holiday. In the 18th and 19th centuries, Bible scholars spurred on by the new study of comparative religions latched on to this idea.[21]

The idea that Christians copied paganism assumes that believers who were still being imprisoned and martyred by Rome somehow decided to adopt the customs of their persecutors. That notion defies both logic and history. It is nonsensical to believe that these same Christians, withstanding persecution from the Roman Empire because of their faith, are at the same time abandoning their faith to participate in – or copy – the festivals and celebrations of the pagan god Saturn. When the evidence is laid out, the myth collapses. It is unthinkable that the same believers who faced prison, fire, and the sword for refusing to bow to Roman gods would suddenly honor those gods in their worship calendar. The sun did not inspire the Son; the Son redefined the sun. Christians celebrated the true Light of the world long before Rome attempted to harness the symbolism of light

---

21. Andrew McGowan, *How December 25 Became Christmas*

for its own political ends. The real "Invincible Son" was never the creation of the empire but the Creator of the universe.

5

Unwrapping Yule

Facts Over Folklore

Another internet myth that dusts off every December is that Christmas was stolen from Yule, the ancient Norse [Norwegian/Scandanavian] winter festival. Scroll through social media and you'll hear that Christians simply rebranded a Viking celebration — that our carols, trees, and feasts all trace back to Odin and his wild ride through the winter sky. It's a claim that sounds convincing, especially to those eager to make Christianity seem like a copycat religion. But once again, the facts tell a far different story.

Let's unwrap the real Yule—not the TikTok version, but the one the Vikings actually celebrated. What you'll see is that Yule and Christmas are not twins. They're not even cousins. Yule wasn't the root of Christmas; it was a completely different thing that got transformed *after* Christianity showed up in the North.

The word *Yule* (Old Norse *jól*, Old English *geol*) likely comes from the same root as words like *wheel* — like Old Norse *hoel* and Anglo-Saxon *hveol*. You can still hear it in modern Icelandic (*hjól*),

Swedish and Danish (*hjul*), and English (*wheel*).[1] That's probably not a coincidence.

Why the connection? Some scholars think it's because the sun was imagined like a wheel — constantly turning through the sky. And at the winter solstice, it "turns back" and begins its climb again, bringing more light each day. So *Yule* may have been a way of marking that solar turning point — when the wheel of the year starts spinning toward spring.

Think of the sun like a giant chariot wheel rolling across the sky. Around the winter solstice, that wheel slows to a stop... and then starts turning back the other way, climbing higher each day. That turning point? The Norse may have called it *jól* — what we now call Yule.

It's not about reindeer or red suits. It's about watching the sun hit rock bottom and then start its comeback — a cosmic "wheel turn" moment. That's likely where the name *Yule* comes from: an ancient word for wheel, symbolizing the shift from darkness to light.

Yule Before Christianity

Old Norse Yule, or *Jól*, happened in the middle of winter—but *not* on December 25. It was tied to the lunar calendar and likely landed in late December or early January. According to *Heimskringla (*a 13th-century saga drawing from earlier oral tradition), before the Christian reforms by King Hákon the Good —a devout Christian raised in

---

1. John M'Clintock and James Strong, "Yule," in Cyclopædia of Biblical, Theological, and Ecclesiastical Literature, Supplement—A–Z (New York: Harper & Brothers, Publishers, 1894), 1012.

DEBUNKING THE PAGAN ROOTS OF CHRISTMAS   79

England[2] — Yule started on midwinter night and lasted three days.[3] Bede mentions two months — 'early Yule' and 'later Yule' — which matched up with Roman December and January. After Christianity came, 'Yule' got narrowed to mean just the nativity (25 Dec) or the 12-day Christmas season.[4] So no, Christmas wasn't "copied" from Yule. They didn't even fall at the same time.

Yule was about sacrifice, drinking, and blessing the gods. People would gather at a local hall or temple, kill animals (even horses), collect the blood in bowls, and sprinkle it on walls, idols, and themselves for blessing. The meat would be boiled and eaten in a massive feast.[5]

They didn't just drink ale—they "drank Yule."[6] The celebration was soaked in mead [honey wine], toasts, and oaths. The first toast went to Odin, asking for victory in battle. The next to Njord and Freyr, for peace and a good harvest. Then came oaths, bold vows, and toasts to dead relatives. It was part war party, part fertility prayer, part ancestral honor.

One standout Yule tradition was the Yule boar. Before the feast, people would lay hands on the boar and swear solemn oaths on its back. Then they sacrificed it, usually to Freyr, a fertility god.[7] That

---

2. Christopher Nichols, "From Jól to Yule," *Scandinavian Archaeology*, December 23, 2021, https://www.scandinavianarchaeology.com/from-jol-to-yule/.

3. Snorri Sturluson, *Heimskringla: History of the Kings of Norway*, trans. Lee M. Hollander (Austin: University of Texas Press, 1964), 76.

4. Jacqueline Simpson and Steve Roud, *A Dictionary of English Folklore* (London, England: Oxford University Press, 2017), 402.

5. Nichols, "From Jól to Yule," under "How?"

6. Ibid, "From Jól to Yule," under "How?"

7. Ibid, under "How" under "How?"

boar shows up later in watered-down form as the Christmas ham or decorative piglets in Scandinavian homes. But the origin? Very pagan. Very bloody.

Yule was also about flexing generosity. *Egil's Saga* tells us about a huge Yule feast hosted by a noble named Arinbjörn, where he gave out lavish Yule-gifts: custom clothes, gold-embroidered robes, the works.[8] Feasting, drinking, storytelling, and gift-giving were all part of the season—not because of baby Jesus, but because that's what Vikings did in winter.

Christianity Rolls In

When Christianity came to Scandinavia in the 10th and 11th centuries, it didn't cancel Yule. It co-opted it. King Hákon the Good of Norway, a Christian raised in England, passed a law: move Yule to match the Christian Christmas. Same party, different reason. Heimskringla [Old Norse for *"Circle of the world"*] explains how King Hákon tried to blend old customs with his new faith:

> King Hákon was a good Christian when he came to Norway; but as the whole country was heathen, with much heathenish sacrifice, and as many great people, as well as the favour of the common people, were to be conciliated, he resolved to practise his Christianity in private. But he kept Sundays, and the Friday fasts, and some token of the greatest holy-days. He made a law that the festival of Yule should begin at the same

---

8. W. C. Green, trans., *Egils Saga* (1893), PDF (Icelandic Saga Database), accessed November 11, 2025, https://sagadb.org/files/pdf/egils_saga.en.pdf., Chapter 70.

> time as Christian people held it, and that every man, under penalty, should brew a meal of malt into ale, and therewith keep the Yule holy as long as it lasted.

> Before him, the beginning of Yule, or the slaughter night, was the night of midwinter (Dec. 14), and Yule was kept for three days thereafter. It was his intent, as soon as he had set himself fast in the land, and had subjected the whole to his power, to introduce Christianity.[9]

That's right. Christians didn't borrow Yule. They let people keep the party *but changed the meaning and date*. It was strategic: don't fight people's favorite feast—just flip it.

Over time, the word *Jól* became the local name for Christmas in Scandinavian countries. Even today, *Jul* means Christmas in Swedish, Norwegian, Danish, and Icelandic. People didn't stop saying "Yule"—they just started saying it about Jesus instead of Odin. This is similar to how *Pascha* became "Easter" in English. In other words, *Yule didn't give birth to Christmas — Christmas gave new meaning to Yule.* What was once a pagan party became a celebration of the Prince of Peace.

The feasting? Kept. The toasts? Kept. The ale? Definitely kept. But now it was done "in honor of Christ" instead of the Norse gods. Sacrifices to Thor and Freyr were outlawed. Horsemeat (sacred to pagan

---

9. Snorri Sturluson, *Heimskringla: History of the Kings of Norway*, trans. Lee M. Hollander (Austin: University of Texas Press, 1964), 75-76.

rites) got banned by Christian kings. Churches replaced temples. The meaning changed, but many customs lived on—repackaged.

The Church had already long established the celebration of Christ's birth on December 25 before it ever reached Scandinavia. When the Norse countries converted, they transferred their midwinter feasting to the Christian holy days. It was a practical strategy: rather than asking converts to give up their favorite festival, the Church blessed it and gave it new meaning. King Hákon's saga makes this strategy explicit – he aligned Yule with "Christian people's" celebration so that his subjects' joyous midwinter feast could continue, but now "in honor of Christ" rather than the heathen gods.

Bottom Line: Christmas Didn't Copy Yule

Yule was a wild, midwinter festival with blood, beer, and boars. It was about honoring Odin, Freyr, and your ancestors. It involved sacrifice, oaths, and seasonal hope. Christmas, on the other hand, was being celebrated on December 25 in Rome as early as the third century—*long before* Scandinavia was even Christian. When the gospel reached the Norse world, Christians didn't borrow Yule. They transformed it. So next time someone says, "Christmas was stolen from Yule," you can say: Nope. Yule got a new name, a new King, and a new reason to celebrate.

6

COUNTERFEIT CHRISTS

EXPOSING THE MYTH OF PAGAN COPYCATS

Every few years, someone dusts off the same tired claim that Christianity is nothing more than a remix of ancient pagan religions—that Jesus is just another version of Osiris, Mithras, or Horus with a new name and updated graphics. But here's the problem: when you actually read the sources, those so-called "similarities" fall apart faster than a cheap counterfeit. The truth is that the Gospel writers weren't borrowing from pagan myths; they were proclaiming fulfilled prophecy.

The ancient world was full of legends about gods who died, descended or came back to life in some symbolic way. But only one story stepped out of myth into history — with eyewitnesses, dates, places, and names you can verify. Christianity didn't copy paganism; it confronted it. When the light of Christ broke into the darkness, the myths didn't fuel the message—they faded in the presence of the real thing.

Horus: The False Parallel

One of the most popular "pagan copycat" myths used against Christianity is the claim that Jesus' birth was copied from Horus. Every Christmas season, memes and internet videos reappear insisting that the story of Jesus is nothing more than a recycled Egyptian myth—that Horus, the falcon-headed god of the Nile, was the "original Jesus." According to these modern claims, Horus was born of a virgin on December 25, heralded by angels, adored by shepherds, baptized, crucified, and resurrected.

It sounds sensational—until you actually read the ancient Egyptian texts. The moment we move from YouTube theology to the historical record, the "Horus = Jesus" argument collapses under its own weight. The real story of Horus bears no meaningful resemblance to the Gospels beyond the obvious fact that both involve a birth and a mother.

In Egyptian mythology, *Horus* was a deity of kingship, protection, and the sky[1] —usually depicted as a man with the head of a falcon.[2] But even "Horus" isn't just one figure. There were *four major versions* of Horus in Egyptian religion:[3]

1. **Horus the Elder** – child of the earth god Geb and sky goddess Nut; brother to Osiris, Isis, and Set.

2. **Horus the Younger** – son of Isis and Osiris, avenger of his father's murder.

---

[1]. John D. Barry et al., eds., "Horus," in *The Lexham Bible Dictionary* (Bellingham, WA: Lexham Press, 2016).

[2]. John W. Klotz, "Birds," in *Baker Encyclopedia of the Bible* (Grand Rapids, MI: Baker Book House, 1988), 352.

[3]. Matt Clayton, *Egyptian Gods: A Captivating Guide to Atum, Horus, Seth, Isis, Anubis, Ra, Thoth, Sekhmet, Geb, Hathor and Other Gods and Goddesses of Ancient Egypt* (Independently Published, 2020), 44.

3. **Ra-Horakhty** – "Ra-Horus of the Double Horizon," merging Horus with the sun god Ra.

4. **Horus of Behdet** – the avenging deity, associated with the midday sun.

These variations show just how fluid and region-specific Egyptian religion was. "Horus" was not one consistent, coherent character but an evolving symbol of royal power and cosmic order. None of these traditions describe an incarnate, historical man born in Bethlehem—or born in any way even remotely close to the Gospels.

Critics love to say Horus was born of a virgin, but most of them have never actually read the ancient Egyptian texts. If they had, they'd never claim that any part of Jesus' story was copied from Horus. Knowing the primary sources—and being able to quote them—is like holding the Big Joker in a game of spades. Once you lay it down, the whole table changes.

Here is what two key Egyptian texts actually say:

The Great Hymn to Osiris (Stela Louvre C286)

The hymn to Osiris is written on a calcite stela—basically a flat, upright stone monument the Egyptians carved with beautiful writing and artwork. It's about three feet tall and two feet wide. This particular stela belonged to a man named Amenmes, an Egyptian who lived during the Eighteenth Dynasty (around 1500–1300 BC).[4] That's the same time period as famous Pharaohs like Thutmose III and King Tut's grandparents. So this hymn isn't from a later copy or a myth

---

4. Stephen E. Thompson, *Ancient Egypt: Facts and Fictions* (Santa Barbara, CA: ABC-CLIO, 2019), 207.

someone made up—it's literally carved in stone from the time of ancient Egypt. It reads:

> Isis the effective, the protecter of her brother, who looked for him without ceasing, who Traveled this land in mourning. she would not rest before she found him. (She) Made a shadow with her feathers, creating a breeze with her wings, offering praise when her brother moored. (She is the one who) lifted up the lethargy of the weary-hearted, who received his semen which created the heir, who suckled the child in solitude, his location was unknown; who revealed him in the court of Geb when he had grown strong. The Ennead rejoices: "Welcome, Osiris' son Horus, stout-hearted, true of voice, son of Isis, heir of Osiris."[5]

We can see in this text Isis' role as the protector of her brother Osiris (yes—her brother and husband) who she returned to life after his murder by Seth. The phrase "lifted up the lethargy of the weary-hearted" is a poetic way of saying that Isis helps Osiris achieve an erection so that he could impregnate her with their son, Horus. And this—this—is the so-called "virgin birth" people claim the Gospels copied.

---

5. *The Great Hymn to Osiris*, trans. S. E. Thompson, after Project Rosette, accessed July 10, 2019, http://projetrosette.info/page.php?Id=799&TextId=18&typeNav=fac&langue=FR#debutTab, quoted in Stephen E. Thompson, *Ancient Egypt: Facts and Fictions* (Santa Barbara, CA: ABC-CLIO, 2019), 209.

Coffin Text Spell 148: The Conception of Horus

Coffin Text Spell 148 is a Middle Kingdom funerary text meant to guide the deceased in the afterlife, and it preserves one of the earliest accounts of Horus' birth. Far from hinting at a virgin birth, this spell describes Isis conceiving Horus only after magically reassembling and reviving Osiris. In other words, the text itself shows that Horus' origin story is rooted in Egyptian mythology, not in anything remotely comparable to the New Testament. It says:

> Isis awakes pregnant with the semen of her brother Osiris. she raises herself up; The woman hastens, her heart pleased with the seamen of her brother Osiris, and she says: "Ho! God's, I am Isis, the sister of Osiris who wept on account of the father of the gods, Osiris, who parted the slaughter of the Two Lands. His semen is inside my body.[6]

Taken together, these primary Egyptian sources make the picture crystal clear: Horus' birth is not a virgin birth. There is no evidence — none — that the New Testament writers were borrowing from, copying, or even influenced by these myths.

To summarize: the Egyptian sources tell the story of Osiris being murdered and dismembered by his brother Set and Isis searching Egypt for his scattered body parts. Finding all but one, she used magic to temporarily reanimate Osiris, fashioning a substitute phallus and

---

6. A. de Buc and A. Gardiner, *The Egyptian Coffin Texts*, vol. 2, trans. S. E. Thompson (Chicago: University of Chicago Press, 1938), 209–226, quoted in Stephen E. Thompson, *Ancient Egypt: Facts and Fictions* (Santa Barbara, CA: ABC-CLIO, 2019), 209.

conceiving Horus through sexual union with her resurrected husband.

After primary sources, one of the best sources we can utilize are Egyptologists, scholars who study the ancient civilization of Egypt, including their history, language, art, and culture. Their verdict is consistent:

- Egyptologist Barbar Lesko (Brown University) notes that "drawings on contemporary funerary papyri show her [Isis] as a kite hovering above Osiris, who is revived enough to have an erection and impregnate his wife."[7]

- Françoise Dunand adds that "after having sexual intercourse, in the form of a bird, with the dead god she restored to life, she gave birth to a posthumous son, Horus."[8]

This isn't a virgin birth—it's divine necromancy. Isis literally revives her deceased husband long enough to conceive. To call this "the same as the virgin birth" is to abandon both logic and language.

The Real Context of Horus' Birth

So how did Horus' birth become associated at all with December 25th? Ancient Egyptian texts like Plutarch's *Moralia* and The *Book of the Dead* place Horus' birth "about the time of the winter solstice," but not on December 25, and not in a manger. Plutarch explains that Isis gave birth to Harpocrates (a Greek form of Horus) "imperfect and

---

7. Barbara S. Lesko, *The Great Goddesses of Egypt the Great Goddesses of Egypt* (Norman, OK: University of Oklahoma Press, 1999), 162.

8. Francoise Dunand and Christiane Zivie-Coche, *Gods and Men in Egypt: 3000 BCE to 395 CE*, trans. David Lorton (Ithaca, NY: Cornell University Press, 2005), 39.

premature" and that "the days of his birth they celebrate after the spring equinox."⁹

Translation: the festival honoring Horus' birth took place *in spring*, not in December.

The whole "December 25 Horus birthday" idea doesn't come from antiquity—it comes from Alexander Hislop's 1850s book *The Two Babylons*,¹⁰ a work that has been debunked by scholars across the theological spectrum. Hislop misquoted sources, retrofitted myths, and invented connections that simply don't exist. We'll address his claims in depth in a later chapter, but for now: Horus was not born on December 25, and no ancient Egyptian text says he was.

The So-Called "Resurrection" of Horus

Horus never dies in the Egyptian myth cycle—not once. It's his father, Osiris, who's murdered, chopped into pieces, scattered across Egypt, magically reassembled, and then installed as the ruler of the underworld. Horus doesn't die and rise again; he grows up to avenge his father's death by throwing hands with Set until justice is restored. His story is about cosmic payback and dynastic legitimacy—not forgiveness, redemption, or new life for humanity.

So when people try to compare Horus to Jesus, the parallel collapses instantly. Horus' myth celebrates vengeance and royal succession; Jesus' story centers on atonement and resurrection. One is a cyclical tale tied to Nile fertility and Egyptian kingship. The other is a once-for-all

---

9. Plutarch, *Moralia*, vol. V: *On Isis and Osiris*, section 65, accessed November 12, 2025, https://penelope.uchicago.edu/Thayer/E/Roman/Texts/Plutarch/Moralia/Isis_and_Osiris*/D.html#T377b.

10. Alexander Hislop, *The Two Babylons* (annotated), Kindle ed., 122.

moment in human history, backed by eyewitness testimony (Luke 24; 1 Cor 15), empty-tomb evidence, and a global movement launched from a single explosion point in time. Horus' story is mythology. Jesus' story is history. And confusing the two says more about someone's research habits than it does about the gospel.

The enduring appeal of the "Horus myth" argument lies not in history but in the hunger for alternatives to divine truth. The human heart longs for redemption, and cultures across time have created symbols of death and renewal. But Christianity doesn't *borrow* that longing—it fulfills it. What Egypt imagined in symbols, God accomplished in history. The myth pointed upward; the Messiah came down. Horus may have ruled the sky, but only Jesus conquered death.

Mithras: The Rock-Born Redeemer That Never Rose

If Horus is the internet's favorite copycat myth, Mithras is the runner-up. Every few years, someone with a microphone, a podcast, or a TikTok filter boldly claims that Jesus is nothing more than a retelling of the Roman god Mithras. According to the myth-makers, Mithras was born of a virgin, had twelve disciples, celebrated a last supper, died for humanity, rose on the third day, and—wait for it—was born on December 25. It's an impressive list... until you actually open the ancient evidence. Because here's the truth: nothing about Mithras matches Jesus. Nothing.

When we set aside the memes and look at the archaeological and literary sources, the "Mithras = Jesus" theory doesn't just fall apart—it evaporates. And once again, primary sources are the Big Joker in this apologetics deck. Let's deal the cards.

Problem #1 - Will The Real Mithras Please Stand Up?

DEBUNKING THE PAGAN ROOTS OF CHRISTMAS 91

The first problem with the Mithras theory is identity. Most critics have no idea which Mithras they're even talking about. Long before the Roman mystery cult ever existed, Mithra was a figure in ancient Indo-Iranian religion—mentioned as early as 1400 BC in treaty inscriptions.[11] In Old Persian, the word "mithra" means "contract." Mithra was regarded as a god who stood for a societal structure based purely on relationships ("contracts") between persons.[12]

This Persian Mithra wasn't a dying-and-rising savior figure; he was the divine enforcer of justice. In the ancient hymns he is the guardian of truth, the god who sees everything, the one whose "long arms" expose liars and whose "eye" watches the world through the sun itself. Mithra assembled warriors, upheld covenants, punished oath breakers, and was associated with rain, health, and the sustaining of life.[13]

For decades, from the late 19th century through the mid-20th, Franz Cumont was the premier authority on Mithraism. Cumont argued that Mithraism stayed mostly the same from its earliest Persian beginnings all the way into the Roman era—a single, unbroken belief system that didn't change much over time. The only problem is, he was wrong.

By the time we get to the Roman Empire of the first through fourth centuries A.D., we're dealing with an entirely different religion—one built around underground initiation rituals, astrological symbolism, and the iconic bull-slaying scene. But there is no indication whatsoever that the Iranian Mithra had anything to do with bulls. Roman Mithra also wasn't interested in contract enforcement or the other things the

---

11. James Patrick Holding, *Shattering the Christ Myth* (Xulon Press, 2008), 203.

12. R. Merkelbach, "Mithras, Mithraism," in *The Anchor Yale Bible Dictionary*, ed. David Noel Freedman (New York: Doubleday, 1992), 877.

13. Holding, *Shattering the Christ Myth*, 203.

previous version of Mithra was known for. In other words, there is no straight line connecting Persian Mithra to Roman Mithras, and certainly no line from either one to Jesus of Nazareth. That's *strike one*.

Problem #2 – A Religion Without Receipts

The second issue is the sheer lack of evidence. Christianity is rooted in texts—Gospels, letters, eyewitness accounts—but Mithraism left behind no scriptures at all. There is no gospel of Mithras. No biography. No sayings. No teachings. No theology. Everything we know about Mithraism comes from cave-shrines, archaeological carvings, inscriptions, and artistic depictions.[14] Cumont admitted that the sacred books of the cult had "vanished and left scarce a trace behind," and that the inner teachings of the cult survive only in a few scattered hints.[15] John Hinnells, another leading expert, remarked that our knowledge of Mithraic rituals and beliefs is "based more on conjecture than fact."[16] In short: critics speak with more certainty about Mithras than the scholars who spent decades excavating his temples. That's strike two.

---

14. Jack Finegan, *Myth and Mystery: An Introduction to the Pagan Religions of the Biblical World* (Grand Rapids: Baker, 1989), 203–7, quoted in Rice Broocks and Travis Thrasher, *Man, Myth, Messiah: Answering History's Greatest Question* (Nashville, TN: W Publishing Group, 2016), 136.

15. Franz Cumont, *The Mysteries of Mithra* (New York: Dover, 1950), 5, quoted in James Patrick Holding, *Shattering the Christ Myth* (Xulon Press, 2008), 204.

16. John R. Hinnells, *Mithraic Studies: Proceedings of the First International Congress of Mithraic Studies* (Manchester University Press, 1975), 437, quoted in James Patrick Holding, *Shattering the Christ Myth* (Xulon Press, 2008), 204.

Problem #3 – Stuck Between A Rock And A Hard Place

The third blow comes from the claim that Mithras was born of a virgin. It sounds impressive on a podcast, but the ancient evidence is completely silent on any mother at all. Every single depiction of Mithras' birth—every carving, every relief—shows him emerging fully grown from a rock. This scene is known as the *petra genetrix*, the "generating rock." Hinnels writes:

> Mithra "wearing his Phrygian cap, issues forth from the Rocky mass. As yet only his bare torso is visible. In each hand he raises aloft a lighted torch and, as an unusual detail, red flames shoot out all around him from the *petra genetix*.[17]

Mithras is shown breaking out of stone, flames bursting around him, wearing his Phrygian cap, holding a torch and dagger — a full grown-up, not anything like a baby in a manger. No woman. No womb. No pregnancy. Just a god stepping out of limestone like a statue coming to life. Calling this a "virgin birth" is like saying a chicken hatching from an egg parallels the Incarnation. The comparison isn't just inaccurate—it's laughable. That's strike three.

Problem #4 – Wrong God, Wrong Date, Wrong Religion

Next comes the December 25 claim. Critics confidently assert that Mithras was born on December 25 and that Christians copied the date. But no ancient Mithraic source ever links Mithras to that day. None. The only Roman deity explicitly tied to December 25 was Sol Invictus, the "Unconquered Sun." And Sol Invictus is not Mithras. Later confusion among writers unfamiliar with the distinctions mud-

---

17. Hinnells, *Mithraic Studies*, quoted in Holding, *Shattering the Christ Myth*, 207.

died the waters, but ancient evidence simply doesn't support the claim. Blomberg details that all alleged associations with the date of December 25 came hundreds of years *after* Christianity:

> Not until the second, third and fourth centuries AD do any noteworthy parallels emerge, such as the celebration of the god's birthday on December 25. And this came about only because the Roman holiday of Saturnalia, not combined with Mithras worship until the second or third century, proved to be a convenient day off work for Christians to worship Jesus and to be left alone to do so...Claims that Christianity or its picture of Jesus was born out of Mithraism reflect almost no historical understanding of chronology, lines of influence, or true similarities and dissimilarities between the two religions.[18]

Even early scholars who studied Mithraism acknowledged that December 25 was widely celebrated as a solstice festival—not a Mithraic birthday.[19] That's strike four.

Problem #5 – Astrology Is Not Apostleship

---

18. Craig L. Blomberg, *The Historical Reliability of the Gospels*, Second Edition (Downers Grove, IL; Nottingham, England: IVP Academic: An Imprint of InterVarsity Press; Apollos, 2007), 138.

19. Franz Cumont, *The Mysteries of Mithra* (New York: Dover, 1950), 196, quoted in James Patrick Holding, *Shattering the Christ Myth* (Xulon Press, 2008), 207.

DEBUNKING THE PAGAN ROOTS OF CHRISTMAS 95

The claim that Mithras had twelve disciples sounds scholarly until you try to find it in the ancient evidence. Then the whole thing collapses like a house built on wet sand. There is no inscription, no relief, no text, no ritual, and no ancient commentary that ever describes Mithras gathering twelve followers who learned from him, traveled with him, or conducted any kind of ministry. The entire idea is a modern invention, and a sloppy one at that.

J. P. Holding exposes this perfectly. He notes that the supposed "twelve disciples of Mithras" comes from a single carved relief in which the famous bull-slaying scene is framed by two vertical rows of six images. That's it. Twelve decorative panels. Nothing in the image identifies these twelve as people, followers, students, or worshipers. But as Holding writes:

> "Freke and Gandy arbitrarily identify these 12 pictures as disciples. Indeed, they go as far as saying that during the Mithraic initiation ceremony, Mithraic disciples dressed up as the signs of the Zodiac and formed a circle around the initiate. Where they get this information about the methods of Mithraic initiation, one can only guess...aside from the fact that this carving is significantly post-Christian (so that any borrowing would have had to be the other way)..."[20]

He goes on to note that "Freke and Gandy attempt to appeal to Joscelyn Godwin's *Mystery Religions in the Ancient World* as their source for Mithras having twelve disciples, yet they provide no page

---

20. Holding, *Shattering the Christ Myth*, 208.

number, and Godwin himself makes no such claim anywhere in his work. In other words: they made it up and hoped nobody would check.

So where does the zodiac actually enter the conversation? Not through discipleship. Not through ritual. Not through any biography of Mithras — because none exists. It comes from astrological symbolism widely used in Roman art. Mithraic reliefs commonly depict: the tauroctony (Mithras slaying the bull), surrounded by

- zodiac symbols representing cosmic order

- constellations such as Leo, Scorpio, Taurus, etc.

This interpretation comes from reputable Mithraic scholars — including David Ulansey (*The Origins of the Mithraic Mysteries*), Roger Beck (Mithraic cosmology expert), and Manfred Clauss (*The Roman Cult of Mithras*). In these works, the zodiac is interpreted as part of Mithraic cosmology, not discipleship. It symbolizes the movement of the heavens and Mithras' role as cosmic lord — not a group of twelve men following a divine teacher.

So yes, twelve symbols appear in Mithraic art — but they are zodiac constellations, not apostles. Critics simply saw the number twelve and forced it into a Christian mold. That's not comparative religion. That's pareidolia — seeing what you want to see. There were no twelve disciples. There were no teachings for them to learn. There was no ministry for them to follow. There was no story for them to enter. When your entire argument rests on misreading a picture frame, that's Strike Five.

Problem #6 – No Tomb, No Third Day, No Comparison

DEBUNKING THE PAGAN ROOTS OF CHRISTMAS

Then there's the most important comparison: the claim that Mithras died and rose again. This is the heart of the Christian message, so if Mithras had anything like it, critics would have a strong case. But Mithras never dies in the ancient evidence. There is no scene of his death, no ritual reenacting it, no inscription describing it, and no resurrection—on the third day or otherwise. Mithraic scholar Richard Gordon emphatically states that there is "no death of Mithras."[21] The central act of Mithras' mythology is his slaying of the cosmic bull, not his own death. You cannot be a "dying and rising god" if you never die. That's strike six.

Problem #7 – A Snack Isn't a Sacrament

Some critics try to salvage the theory by pointing to the Mithraic communal meal, suggesting it mirrors the Christian Eucharist. But the differences are striking:

> The closest thing that Mithraism had to a Last Supper was the taking of staples (bread, water, wine, and meat) by the Mithraic initiates, Which was perhaps a celebration of the meal that Mithra had with the sun deity after slaying the bull. However, the meal of the initiates is evidently no more than a general fellowship meal of the sort that was practiced by groups all over the Roman world – from religious groups to funereal societies.[22]

---

21. Richard Gordon, *Image and Value in the Greco-Roman World* (Aldershot: Variorum, 1996), cited in J. P. Holding, *Shattering the Christ Myth*, 210.

22. Holding, *Shattering The Christ Myth*, 211.

The Mithraic meal was a secret banquet for initiated men, not an open call to repentant sinners. It had no language of covenant, no symbolism of "body and blood," no theology of atonement, and no connection to any sacrificial death—because Mithras never died in the first place. Sharing bread and wine does not make a religion parallel to Christianity any more than sharing food makes Thanksgiving equivalent to Passover. That's strike seven.

Conclusion

The Mithras theory survives today for one simple reason: it gives people an escape hatch from the claims of Jesus. If the gospel can be reduced to another recycled myth, then Christ's resurrection can be dismissed, His authority ignored, and His call to repentance conveniently avoided. But when you bring the ancient evidence to the table—and lay down that primary-source Big Joker—the entire argument folds on the spot. Mithras never lived as a historical person, never taught the crowds, never healed the sick, never died for anyone, and never rose again. His cult left carvings and symbols in underground caves; Jesus left an empty tomb and eyewitnesses willing to die rather than deny what they saw. One faith was built on secrecy; the other was launched in broad daylight. One was centered on a cosmic bull-slayer; the other on the Lamb of God who takes away the sin of the world. When the dust settles, the contrast is unmistakable. Mithras is mythology. Jesus is Lord.

Dionysus: Receipts vs. Rumors

Dionysus is another one of the most frequently cited "pagan prototypes" critics try to tie to Jesus. The claims float around like recycled

DEBUNKING THE PAGAN ROOTS OF CHRISTMAS

urban legends — Dionysus was born of a virgin, died and rose on March 25, turned water into wine, offered his followers communion, and inspired Christian sacramental theology. It sounds impressive until you stop believing rumors and start checking receipts. Because the moment you consult the ancient sources, every single alleged parallel falls apart.

Dionysus is not a pagan Christ. He isn't even close. He's the Greek god of wine and ecstatic experience generally, and to some extent also of vegetation, and of death and rebirth. He was also remarkable as being subject to birth (from a mortal woman), death, and resurrection.[23] The evidence will show that He is a far cry from the incarnate, crucified, risen Savior revealed in history. In many ways Dionysus is a God of paradox; he was a god of fertility, but also a God who comforted the dying. He is depicted sometimes as a maniacal, destructive figure, and at other times as an innocent child; sometimes as a bearded man, other times as an effeminate youth. Let's follow the trail of rumors — and then check the receipts.

Rumor #1: Dionysus Was Virgin-Born.

Receipt: His Birth Story Begins With Zeus' Lust, Not Virginity.

A great deal of the information we know about Dionysus that is used by proponents of the copycat theory comes from story from the Greek playwright Euripides called "The Bacchae." The Bacchae is a Greek tragedy about Dionysus returning to his birthplace of Thebes to exact vengeance on the arrogant King Pentheus, who refuses to acknowledge his divinity. The play culminates in divine retribution as

---

23. John M. Dillon, "Dionysus (Deity)," in *The Anchor Yale Bible Dictionary*, ed. David Noel Freedman (New York: Doubleday, 1992), 201.

Dionysus drives Pentheus's mother and her sisters into a mad frenzy, causing them to tear the king limb from limb

Nothing in Greek mythology about Dionysus even hints at a virgin birth. His most well-known origin story begins when the god Zeus has an affair and impregnates his lover Semele when he took the form of a lightning bolt. The text from the Bacchae reads: "Casting him from her stomach as she was struck by Zeus' thunder while in the compulsions of birth pains, leaving life from the stroke of a thunderbolt."[24]

There is no virginity involved — just divine seduction and jealousy-driven tragedy. Hera, Zeus' wife, manipulates Semele into asking Zeus to reveal his glory, which ends up burning Semele away, leaving the prenatal Dionysus behind. Zeus rescues the fetus and literally sews Dionysus into his thigh until he is ready to be born.[25] This is where his title "twice-born" comes from — not from a miraculous conception, but from surviving the chaos of divine adultery.

Other Greek variants claim Dionysus was conceived by Zeus and Persephone.[26] Yet another Asiatic version has Dionysus self-born.[27] None of them involve a virgin. All of them involve gods behaving badly. Calling this a "virgin birth" is like calling a lightning strike a baptism. The receipt is clear: no virginity, no parallel.

Rumor #2: Dionysus Died and Rose on March 25.

---

24. Euripides, *The Bacchae*, trans. T. A. Buckley, rev. Alex Sens, further rev. Gregory Nagy, accessed November 12, 2025, https://www.uh.edu/~cldue/texts/bacchae.html.

25. Dillon, *Dionysus (Deity)*, 201.

26. Arthur Evans, *The God of Ecstasy: Sex-Roles and the Madness of Dionysos* (New York: St. Martin's Press, 1988), quoted in James Patrick Holding, *Shattering the Christ Myth* (Xulon Press, 2008), 233.

27. Holding, *Shattering The Christ Myth*, 233.

DEBUNKING THE PAGAN ROOTS OF CHRISTMAS 101

Receipt: There Is No Resurrection Narrative — Only Seasonal Symbolism

Skeptics confidently point to March 25 as Dionysus' "resurrection day," but there's not a single ancient text that says Dionysus died, was buried, or rose again on any date — let alone the one associated with Jesus. Classical scholar Susan Cole notes: "I have found no evidence to support the 'March 25th' claim."[28] She adds that the *only* inscription linking Dionysus to "renewal" comes from Thasos, where he is described as a god who rejuvenates annually.[29] But she immediately adds that the context is unclear — it likely refers to vegetation cycles, not bodily resurrection.

This is ancient agrarian symbolism, not historical resurrection. Seeds "die" and return in spring. Harvests "rise" after winter. But no Greek worshiper confused Dionysus' vegetative renewal with the return of a crucified Messiah. The rumor says resurrection. The receipt says seasonal metaphor.

Rumor #3: Dionysus Was a Dying-and-Rising Savior God.

Receipt: He Never Lived in History, Never Died for Sin, and Never Rose.

The so-called "dying and rising gods" of the ancient world are almost entirely symbolic — and Dionysus is Exhibit A. He never lived as a historical figure. There is no crucifixion. No burial. No empty tomb. No witnesses. No third day. No conquered grave.

---

28. Ibid, 234.

29. Susan Guettel Cole, "12. Voices from beyond the Grave: Dionysus and the Dead". Masks of Dionysus, edited by Thomas H. Carpenter and Christopher A. Faraone, Ithaca, NY: Cornell University Press, 1993, 280. https://doi.org/10.7591/9781501733680-017

At most, Dionysus represents vegetation cycles: grapevines that "die," wineskins that ferment, harvests that return. But this isn't resurrection — it's agricultural poetry. Ancient Greeks did not look to Dionysus for salvation, forgiveness, or eternal life. They looked to him for wine, frenzy, and emotional release. The rumor invents a resurrection. The receipt proves none ever existed.

Receipts vs. Rumors: The Final Word on Dionysus

Dionysus is not a prototype for Christ. He is not a pagan foreshadowing. He is not a mythic Messiah. The virgin birth of the pagan god Dionysus is attested only in post-Christian sources. It is significant that it is indeed Christians who speak of his virgin birth, but only several centuries after Christ.[30] Every alleged parallel — virgin birth, atonement, resurrection, communion, miracle-working — collapses under the weight of evidence the moment you check the receipts. Dionysus was a mythic figure of intoxication and ecstasy. Jesus is the incarnate Son of God who entered history, died for sin, and rose again. One points to wine. The other points to the cross. Only one leaves an empty tomb behind. Rumors may circulate. But the receipts tell the truth.

Krishna: The Case That Falls Apart Under Cross-Examination

---

30. J. Ed Komoszewski, M. James Sawyer, and Daniel B. Wallace, *Reinventing Jesus: How Contemporary Skeptics Miss the Real Jesus and Mislead Popular Culture* (Grand Rapids, MI: Kregel Publications, 2006), 242.

DEBUNKING THE PAGAN ROOTS OF CHRISTMAS

If skeptics were building a courtroom case that Christianity copied pagan mythology, Krishna is often their star witness — the one they confidently put on the stand as their "smoking gun." They repeat the same list of allegations: Krishna was virgin-born, performed miracles, died for humanity, rose from the dead, and ascended into heaven before Jesus supposedly arrived and stole the story. The rumors are bold. But when you bring the primary sources into the courtroom and place them under oath, the testimony tells a very different story. This isn't a trial where Krishna supports the prosecution. This is a trial where Krishna becomes Exhibit A in the failure of the entire pagan-parallels argument.

Exhibit A: The Alleged Virgin Birth

The prosecution claims Krishna was conceived of a virgin. But the official court record from the Mahabharata, the Harivamsa, and the testifies otherwise. The Harivamsa is a key Sanskrit text that serves as a supplement or appendix (khila) to the ancient Indian epic, the *Mahabharata*. It primarily focuses on the detailed genealogy of the Yadava clan and the life story, childhood exploits, and divine activities of Lord Krishna. It details the story of Krishna's mother, Devaki, a married woman. She conceived children with her husband Vasudeva through normal human relations and bore seven children before Krishna.[31] The text says that Devakī conceived Krishna in the ordinary way, and that his birth occurred in a prison where she and Vasudeva were held by her tyrant brother, Kaṁsa. Fearing a prophecy that Devakī's eighth

---

31. Manmatha Nath Dutt, *A Prose English Translation of Harivaṁśa*, trans. (Calcutta: H. C. Dass, 1897), chap. LIX, "Birth of Krishna and Baladeva," accessible at Project Gutenberg, https://www.gutenberg.org/cache/epub/61937/pg61937-images.html#chapter-lix-birth-of-krishna-and-baladeva.

child would destroy him, Kaṁsa imprisoned them and killed their first six children. Krishna, the eighth child, is miraculously protected after birth—but there is no claim of virginity in his conception or pregnancy.

The Bhāgavata Purāṇa, one of Hinduism's most influential devotional texts, contains the most detailed version of Krishna's birth, yet it offers no suggestion of a virgin birth. Written centuries after the New Testament, this Purāṇa describes Krishna being conceived and born to Devakī and her husband Vasudeva in a prison cell, with Devakī explicitly called Vasudeva's wife and mother of multiple children. The text repeatedly emphasizes that Krishna enters Devakī's womb and is then born as her son:

> Then the Supreme Personality of Godhead, Viṣṇu, who is situated in the core of everyone's heart, appeared from the heart [womb] of Devakī in the dense darkness of night, like the full moon rising on the eastern horizon, because Devakī was of the same category as Śrī Kṛṣṇa. Vasudeva then saw the newborn child, who had very wonderful lotuslike eyes and who bore in His four hands the four weapons śaṅkha, cakra, gadā and padma...When Vasudeva saw his extraordinary son, his eyes were struck with wonder.[32]

---

32. *Bhāgavata Purāṇa* 10.3.7, trans. A. C. Bhaktivedanta Swami Prabhupāda, Vedabase, https://vedabase.io/en/library/sb/10/3/7-11/.

A divine incarnation, yes, but not a virginal conception. Nothing in the Bhāgavata Purāṇa parallels the Christian doctrine of the virgin birth.

The prosecution points to myths and late devotional poetry as if they were sworn testimony, but the primary sources speak clearly. In Bhāgavata Purāṇa 10.3.7-11, Devakī is identified as the *mother-figure* and Vasudeva as the father figure (10.3.13), thus affirming Krishna's birth from two human parents — not the incarnation of the Son of God through the overshadowing of the Holy Spirit. No virgin. No Annunciation. No miracle. Exhibit A is dismissed.

Exhibit B: The Angelic Announcement That Wasn't

Next, critics insist Krishna's birth was heralded by divine messengers just like Jesus. But when we review the evidence, what they call "angels" turns out to be nothing more than a political prophecy: King Kamsa receives a warning that Devaki's eighth child will end his reign. The text declares: "Even if Kaṁsa were to see that the eighth child of Devakī was a daughter, he should have no doubt that the eighth child was to kill him."[33] That's it. No heavenly choir. No shepherds. No angelic proclamation. Just a frightened tyrant reacting to a seer's message. This is far closer to Pharaoh fearing Moses than Gabriel announcing Jesus. The prosecution has mistaken a royal panic for divine revelation. Exhibit B is irrelevant to the case.

The Verdict on Krishna

---

33. *Śrīmad-Bhāgavatam*, Canto 10, chap. 1, verse 34, trans. A. C. Bhaktivedanta Swami Prabhupāda, Vedabase, https://vedabase.io/en/library/sb/10/1/34/.

When Krishna's story is examined in the courtroom of historical evidence, every alleged parallel to Jesus collapses. The virgin birth is absent. The resurrection is nonexistent. The communion is imaginary. The miracles don't align. And the purpose of Krishna's incarnation — restoring cosmic order, not redeeming humanity — couldn't be further from the gospel. The verdict is clear: Krishna is not a prototype for Christ. He is a mythic avatar in a completely different universe of meaning. The prosecution rests — because it has no case left to make.

The Bootleg Messiahs: Buddha, Attis, and Zoroaster

Not every supposed "copycat Christ" deserves a full trial. Some claims are so thin that they belong in the bargain bin of ideas — the mythological bootlegs that crumble the moment you check the stitching. These figures get name-dropped in memes and documentaries, but the receipts show they're not even in the same genre as Jesus. They're the theological equivalent of knockoff sneakers: similar colors from far away, but all the details fall apart on inspection. Below are three of the most common "bootleg Messiahs" skeptics throw into the mix — and why none of them stand up next to the Original.

Buddha: The Philosophy Remix That Isn't a Messiah

People love to claim that Jesus is just a remix of Buddha — but the moment you check the label, you realize these two are in completely different categories. Buddha was born to Suddhodana, king of Kapilavastu, in 557 B.C.[34] In the story of Buddha's conception,

---

34. Samuel Macauley Jackson, ed., *The New Schaff-Herzog Encyclopedia of Religious Knowledge* (New York; London: Funk & Wagnalls, 1908–1914), 292.

nothing is said of a date of December 25 or angels. Two dates, the 8th day of the 4th lunar month (Date A) and the 8th day of the 2nd lunar month (Date B), are found in Chinese Buddhist translations as the Buddha's birthday.[35]

Buddha isn't a savior; he's a philosopher and moral teacher. He didn't die for sins; he taught a way of life called the Eightfold Path — a set of eight disciplines (right belief, right intention, right speech, right conduct, right livelihood, right effort, right mindfulness, and right concentration) designed to help people escape suffering through self-mastery. And he didn't rise from the dead; he achieved what Buddhism calls nirvana, the extinguishing of desire and release from the cycle of rebirth — not resurrection, and certainly not victory over death.

His origin story isn't a virgin birth either. Queen Maya was married, conceived naturally, and delivered a historical child whose life is framed by symbolic dreams, not divine incarnation. Jesus brings redemption. Buddha brings reflection. One offers atonement; the other offers advice. Buddha is profound. But he's not a Messiah — he's the philosophy remix, not the Savior original. Trying to make him a prototype for Christ is like confusing a TED Talk with an empty tomb.

Attis: The Seasonal Loop, Not the Resurrection

Attis is often marketed online as the "dying and rising god" that Jesus supposedly imitates, but once you check the stitching, he turns out to be a seasonal remix, not a resurrection original. In the ancient Phry-

---

35. Meiqiao Zhang, "Whence the 8th Day of the 4th Lunar Month as the Buddha's Birthday," *Religions* 14, no. 4 (2023): 451, https://doi.org/10.3390/rel14040451.

gian myth, Attis dies in a frenzy beneath a pine tree after mutilating himself — a tragic collapse tied to his devotion to the goddess Cybele.

> Zeus (as Jupiter) saw Mt. Agdus, which looked like the goddess Rhea, and dropped some of his seed on the mountain, creating a wild creature named Agdistis, whom the gods do not like. So Dionysus sneaks up and puts wine in Agdistis' water to put him to sleep and ties a rope around his genitals, tying the other end of the rope to a tree, and then frightens him awake. The panic causes Agdistis to castrate himself. From the resulting blood, a tree springs up, and much later, Nana happens by, picks some of the fruit, and puts it in her lap and then it disappears – upon which, she finds herself pregnant with Attis.[36]

Ancient worshipers connected Attis to the rhythms of springtime, where vegetation dies in winter and reappears in spring. In other words, Attis symbolizes cyclical nature, not a historical resurrection.

Zoroaster: The Prophet With a Preview, Not the Prototype

Zoroaster (or Zarathustra) gets thrown into the mix as if he were the early draft of Jesus, but that's only because critics are reading headlines instead of history. Zoroaster wasn't virgin-born. He didn't claim divinity. He didn't die a sacrificial death or rise again. What he offered was ethical dualism — a worldview in which the universe is

---

36. M. J. Bermaseren, *Cybele and Attis: The Myth and the Cult* (London: Thames and Hudson, 1977), 4, 9

locked in a moral conflict between Ahura Mazda (the Wise Lord) and Angra Mainyu (the evil spirit). His mission wasn't to redeem sinners but to call people to align with truth, order, and righteousness in that cosmic struggle.

Our main source for details on Zoroaster is the *Avesta*, a collection of sacred text which was put in writing between 346 – 360 A.D. and of which we have manuscript copies only as early as the 13th century.[37] The Avesta refers to a "kingly glory" that was handed onward from one ruler to the next. This glory resided in Zoroaster's mother for about 15 years, including during the time she was married to Zoroaster's father, Pourushaspa. It seems that a human father was still needed for Zoroaster and that this "Ray" was merely for the infusion of Zoroaster's spirit, not his body.[38] Zoroaster brought wisdom. Jesus brought salvation. One proclaimed cosmic ethics; the other conquered the grave. They are not parallels — they are universes apart.

Serapis: The Meme That Became a Myth

Every now and then, a claim pops up online insisting that early Christians actually worshiped Serapis — as if Jesus were just a knockoff of a Greco-Egyptian hybrid deity. But when you look at the receipts, Serapis isn't a Christ-parallel at all; he's a political remix created by the Ptolemies to unify Greeks and Egyptians under one religious banner. As one historian explains, *"Serapis was a conflation of the healing*

---

37. Ernst Herzfeld, *Zoroaster and His World* (Octagon Books, 1974), 774; John Waterhouse, *Zoroastrianism* (Epworth, n.d.), 56, quoted in James Patrick Holding, *Shattering The Christ Myth* (Bloomington, IN: Xulon Press, 2008), 212.

38. A. V. W. Jackson, *Zoroaster the Prophet of Ancient Iran* (New York: AMS Press, 1965), 18, 24.

attributes of the god Apis with the resurrection, agriculture, and underworld connections of Osiris."[39] In other words, he was a government-sponsored mash-up — not a virgin-born savior, not a redeemer, not a teacher, and not a resurrected Lord. His myths have nothing resembling the gospel: no incarnation, no atonement, no cross, no empty tomb. Serapis was a state-issued symbol meant to stabilize a multicultural empire, not a Messiah who came to save sinners.

So where did the Jesus/Serapis rumor come from? Not antiquity — the 1800s. The entire idea traces back to one misused line from a sarcastic comment attributed to Emperor Hadrian in the *Historia Augusta*, where he mocks Egyptians for mixing every religion into one big theological stew.[40] Hadrian wasn't saying Christians worshiped Serapis; he was ridiculing Alexandrian religious chaos. But in 1829, Robert Taylor ripped this satire out of context in *The Diegesis* and used it to claim Christianity evolved from Serapis worship.[41] No church father believed this. No pagan critic argued it. No historian supports it. Serapis isn't a prototype for Jesus — he's the bootleg of a bootleg, a meme-powered myth built on a single line that ancient readers understood as a joke. When held next to the gospel, Serapis doesn't look like the original; he looks like the counterfeit people reach for when they haven't checked the source material.

---

39. Margaret Froelich, "Serapis," in The Lexham Bible Dictionary, ed. John D. Barry et al. (Bellingham, WA: Lexham Press, 2016).

40. *Historia Augusta*, "The Life of Saturninus," in Scriptores Historiae Augustae, trans. David Magie, vol. 3, Loeb Classical Library 263 (Cambridge, MA: Harvard University Press, 1932), 399.

41. Robert Taylor, *The Diegesis: Being a Discovery of the Origin, Evidences, and Early History of Christianity* (London: R. Carlile, 1829), 407.

Closing Summary: Myths Fade When the Light Hits Them

When you line up every so-called "pagan parallel" next to the story of Jesus, the truth becomes unmistakable: none of them even come close. Horus wasn't virgin-born. Mithras never died. Dionysus didn't rise. Krishna wasn't crucified. Buddha never claimed to be God. Attis symbolizes the seasons, not salvation. Zoroaster pointed forward to cosmic hope, not an empty tomb. Serapis is a modern internet myth, not an ancient rival. Every alleged resemblance collapses the moment you check the receipts instead of repeating the rumors.

These myths move in circles — symbolic rebirth, seasonal cycles, spiritual enlightenment, cosmic struggle — but none of them break into history with a named mother, a dated census, a real city, political leaders you can place on a timeline, eyewitnesses who recorded what they saw, and a resurrection that launched a movement the Roman Empire could not crush. The story of Jesus is not a remix of ancient mythology; it is the moment God entered human history, fulfilling prophecy, confronting darkness, and inaugurating redemption.

And here's the irony no skeptic ever mentions: If any borrowing happened, it wasn't Christians copying pagans — it was pagans reshaping their stories after Jesus. Many of the "parallels" skeptics point to appear *after* the spread of Christianity, not before it. The timeline doesn't support the copycat theory; it exposes it. Myths adjust, religions adapt, symbols shift — but the gospel remains rooted in time, space, and verifiable history.

Christmas was not borrowed from Egypt, Persia, Greece, India, or Rome. It was not plagiarized from Horus, Mithras, Dionysus, Attis, Krishna, or anyone else.

Christmas exists because a real Child was born, in a real place, at a real moment, just as the prophets said, to bring a kind of hope no myth ever offered. Myths echo human longing. Jesus fulfills it. Myths rise and fall. Jesus rose — and still reigns. That is why, two thousand years later...every copycat fades, but Christ remains the Original.

7

THE MAN BEHIND THE MYTH

HOW ALEXANDER HISLOP CREATED A PAGAN CHRISTMAS

Once you peel back every modern claim that Christmas or Easter is "pagan," you eventually find yourself staring at the same name: Alexander Hislop. If the previous chapter exposed the so-called pagan "copycats," this chapter exposes the man who unintentionally became the architect of the entire myth-making industry behind them. Hislop is the invisible hand behind almost every argument you hear on social media today. When someone argues that Christmas came from Nimrod, that the Christmas tree represents Tammuz, that December 25 is Babylonian, that Easter comes from Ishtar, or that Catholic tradition is built on paganism, they are not quoting ancient history — they are quoting Hislop, usually without realizing it.

The problem is that Hislop wasn't a historian or an archaeologist. He wrote before most of what we now know about the ancient Near East had been excavated or translated. But even for his time, his method was reckless. Instead of starting with evidence and forming conclusions, he began with a conclusion — "Rome is Babylon"

— and forced every scrap of mythology he could find to support it.[1] His book, *The Two Babylons*, originally a pamphlet published in 1853, expanded into a sweeping accusation that everything in Roman Catholicism descended from ancient Babylonian religion. Not "some things," not "a few rituals," but everything. It was a global conspiracy theory in print, long before the internet made such things fashionable.

Hislop's method was simple: if two things looked vaguely similar, he declared them identical. He jumped across thousands of years and entire civilizations, claiming that any resemblance — a symbol, a name, a seasonal festival, a ritual gesture — proved direct borrowing. Modern scholars call this *parallelomania*, the habit of forcing parallels where none exist. But Hislop built entire chapters out of it. If a word in one language *sounded* like a name in another, he claimed they shared a common root. If a goddess somewhere in the world had a trait in common with another goddess, he insisted they were identical. His logic was so loose that it would be like claiming "hamburger" came from "Ham," the son of Noah, simply because the words share a syllable.

One of Hislop's favorite targets was Tammuz, the Mesopotamian figure behind many of his most dramatic claims. Tammuz was an ancient Near Eastern god whose story resembles the later Greek myth of Adonis. He began as a Sumerian/Babylonian figure named Dumuzu, the husband of Ishtar (who the Greeks later associated with Aphrodite). Worship of Tammuz and Ishtar spread early into places like Syria, where they were known as Tammuz and Astarte. Later, when the Greeks encountered these older traditions, they didn't believe Tammuz and Ishtar turned into Adonis and Aphrodite—rather,

---

1. Hislop, *The Two Babylons*, Kindle ed., loc. 101.

they recognized similarities and connected their own gods to them.[2] The same happened in Egypt, where people drew parallels between these stories and the myths of Osiris and Isis. All of this shows how widespread and comparable these ancient religious traditions became across cultures.

In Hislop's version, Tammuz becomes the root of Christmas trees, winter festivals, resurrection myths, and even December 25 itself. But none of this comes from genuine ancient Near Eastern sources. The real Tammuz (Dumuzi in Sumerian, meaning "good son"[3]) was a shepherd deity associated with agricultural cycles and seasonal lament[4] — not a winter god, not a resurrected savior, and certainly not a proto-Christ. Nothing in cuneiform tablets, Mesopotamian mythology, or archaeological record connects Tammuz to the date of December 25, evergreen trees, gift-giving, or the incarnation. Hislop stitched together unrelated myths, misunderstood languages he didn't speak, and filled in the gaps with imagination. It was compelling storytelling, not historical research.

Hislop's conclusions were also driven by circular reasoning. He began by assuming that Babylon was the fountainhead of all false religion. He assumed Catholicism was a false religion. Therefore, Catholicism must come from Babylon.[5] Every similarity then became proof of his assumption, and every myth he encountered became

---

2. H. Porter, "Tammuz," in *The International Standard Bible Encyclopaedia*, ed. James Orr et al. (Chicago: The Howard-Severance Company, 1915), 2908.

3. Sara Wells, https://ref.ly/logosres/lbd?art=tammuz_deity&off=157&ctx=logy+and+Background%0a~The+name+Tammuz+deri in *The Lexham Bible Dictionary*, ed. John D. Barry et al. (Bellingham, WA: Lexham Press, 2016).

4. H. Porter, "Tammuz," 2908.

5. Hislop, "The Two Babylons," Kindle ed., loc. 127.

evidence of his conclusion. It was an echo chamber bound in hardcover. And because archaeology was still in its infancy, there were few scholars available to correct him, and even fewer resources to evaluate his claims. He wrote before the discovery of major ancient cities like Nineveh, Ugarit, Mari, and Ebla — places that would eventually reveal the real history of the ancient Near East and disprove almost everything he wrote.

Yet Hislop's book spread like wildfire. It was bold, dramatic, and written with the confidence of someone who believed he had uncovered a global conspiracy. His work influenced anti-Catholic writers, fringe religious groups, conspiracy theorists, and, in the modern era, YouTube channels and TikTok influencers who repeat Hislop's claims without ever checking a single ancient source. Hislop's voice echoes everywhere today — but only because people quote him secondhand, assuming he is passing on ancient knowledge when in reality he was guessing in the dark.

And that is why Hislop matters for the Christmas debate. Virtually every modern claim that Christmas or Easter has pagan roots — that December 25 is Babylonian, that the Christmas tree is pagan, that Santa is a repackaged deity, that Mary and Jesus copy Ishtar and Tammuz — can be traced directly back to Hislop's pen. His conclusions spread far beyond their original anti-Catholic context and ended up shaping entire corners of Christian culture and internet skepticism alike. But once you dig past the claims and into the historical evidence, Hislop's foundation crumbles. His work was not based on ancient texts, archaeology, or linguistics. It was based on assumptions held together by creative parallels, but it's time to set the record straight.

Dismantling Hislop: The Myth of Tammuz, December 25, and the Christmas Tree

One of Hislop's boldest claims is that Tammuz was born on December 25 and that this Babylonian festival was the true origin of Christmas. In his words: "the festival of Tammuz was celebrated at the winter solstice...[6] his birthday was observed on December 25th".[7] This one line has been repeated in countless sermons, YouTube videos, and internet debates. Yet the trouble begins immediately — because Hislop never cites a single ancient source for this claim, and the claim is contradicted by every real piece of Mesopotamian evidence we possess.

Archaeology reveals a completely different picture. Tammuz (Dumuzi) was a Sumerian shepherd god associated with seasonal agriculture, not winter festivals. His death was lamented in the late spring or early summer, and his "revival" reflected nothing more than the return of vegetation cycles.[8] Dumuzi's myth is tied to "hot, dry summer months – explained in mythology as being caused by Tammuz's death and descent into the underworld. His followers would weep, mourn his death, and in the spring Tammuz would emerge victoriously from the underworld and bring with him the life-giving rains.[9] So the evidence demonstrates that Tammuz was associated with summer—not

---

6. Hislop, "The Two Babylons," Kindle ed., loc. 2496.

7. Ibid, loc. 2481.

8. Lowell K. Handy, "Tammuz (Deity)," in *The Anchor Yale Bible Dictionary*, ed. David Noel Freedman (New York: Doubleday, 1992), 318.

9. Charles H. Dyer, https://ref.ly/logosres/bkc?ref=Bible.Eze8.14-15&off=553&ctx=e ath.+In+the+spring+~Tammuz+would+emerge+ in *The Bible Knowledge Commentary: An Exposition of the Scriptures*, ed. J. F. Walvoord and R. B. Zuck, vol. 1 (Wheaton, IL: Victor Books, 1985), 1244.

the winter solstice or December celebrations. There is zero evidence in any cuneiform tablet linking Tammuz to December 25 (or any winter observance), and not a single Babylonian text places his birth or festival anywhere near the solstice.

Even Hislop's attempted evidence collapses. He tries to connect Tammuz to a claim that "the son of Isis was born about the time of the winter solstice,"[10] arguing that Horus = Tammuz and thus December 25 must be Babylonian. But when the actual source he cites is checked (Wilkinson's *Ancient Egyptians*, vol. 4, 405.), the text does not refer to Horus at all — it refers to Harpocrates, who was considered a premature infant, and whose feast was celebrated in spring, not winter.[11] Plutarch confirms this:

> For this reason also it is said that Isis, when she perceived that she was pregnant, put upon herself an amulet on the sixth day of the month Phaophi; and about the time of the winter solstice she gave birth to Harpocrates, imperfect and premature, amid the early flowers and shoots. For this reason they bring to him as an offering the first-fruits of growing lentils, and the days of his birth they celebrate after the spring equinox.[12]

---

10. Hislop, "The Two Babylons," Kindle ed., loc. 2496.

11. Ralph Woodrow, "*The Two Babylons: A Case Study in Poor Methodology*," *Christian Research Journal*, April 9, 2009, accessed November 15, 2025, https://www.equip.org/articles/the-two-babylons/

12. Plutarch, *Moralia: Volume V, "On Isis and Osiris"* (§ 65),

Harpocrates was the son of Isis referenced and the days of his birth were celebrated after the spring equinox, not on December 25. In other words, Hislop misread his source, misidentified the deity, and then misapplied the conclusion — three errors in a single argument.

The same pattern repeats with Hislop's claim that the Christmas tree comes from the worship of Tammuz. Hislop insists that the decorated tree was a Babylonian emblem of the resurrected god.[13] Many turn to Jeremiah 10 and insist it is a reference to Christmas trees.

> For the customs of the peoples are worthless. Someone cuts down a tree from the forest; it is worked by the hands of a craftsman with a chisel. He decorates it with silver and gold. It is fastened with hammer and nails, so it won't totter. (Jer 10:3-4 CSB)

The context makes it clear that Jeremiah 10 describes carved wooden idols, not evergreen trees; the passage explicitly says the wood is shaped by a craftsman and fastened so it will not topple — a description that does not match a Christmas tree in any way. We will address this further in a subsequent chapter.

No Babylonian myth or ritual text connects evergreen trees to Tammuz. The Christmas tree, as documented in medieval sources, arises more than two thousand years later in Christian Europe, shaped by Paradise plays, medieval symbolism, and folk tradition — not Babylonian religion.

Modern scholarship — which Hislop never had access to — makes Hislop's mistakes obvious. Thousands of excavated tablets confirm

---

13. Hislop, "The Two Babylons," Kindle ed., loc. 2585.

Tammuz's association with summer, fertility, and agricultural cycles. Nothing connects him to winter, solstice, December festivals, or evergreens. Hislop's claims do not originate from ancient texts; they originate from parallelomania — the practice of drawing lines between unrelated ideas simply because they "look similar" from a distance.

Hislop began with a conclusion ("Christmas is pagan") and then handpicked anything that sounded vaguely parallel, regardless of chronology, geography, language, or primary evidence. In the case of Tammuz and December 25, the factual record is clear: Hislop's argument collapses the moment the ancient sources are opened. His solstice theory is not archaeology, linguistics, or history — it's nineteenth-century speculation masquerading as scholarship.

Dismantling the Nimrod–Semiramis–Tammuz Myth

Hislop's entire theory stands or falls on a single claim: that Nimrod, Semiramis, and Tammuz formed an ancient Babylonian "holy family" whose worship later "evolved" into Catholicism and then into modern Christmas. He states plainly:

> How, then, did the Romish Church fix on December the 25th as Christmas-day? Why, thus: Long before the fourth century, and long before the Christian era itself, a festival was celebrated among the heathen, at that precise time of the year, in honour of the birth of the son [Tammuz] of the Babylonian queen of heaven [Ishtar]; and it may fairly be presumed that, in order to conciliate the heathen, and to swell the number of the nominal adherents of Christianity, the same festival

DEBUNKING THE PAGAN ROOTS OF CHRISTMAS 121

was adopted by the Roman Church, giving it only the name of Christ.[14]

So Hislop presumes that Nimrod was the father, Semiramis the mother, and Tammuz the son — a trinity he then projects onto nearly every culture in the ancient world. But the problem is as simple as it is devastating: **this trio never existed together in any ancient text.** Not in Babylon. Not in Assyria. Not in Sumer. Not in any archaeological inscription, myth cycle, or king list.

Nimrod is a figure appearing briefly in Genesis 10:8–12. Scripture describes him as a mighty hunter and the founder of certain Mesopotamian cities. That is all. Every historical reconstruction places Nimrod — if he is linked to any historical figure — somewhere in the early second millennium BC, possibly connected to Sargon of Akkad or other early Mesopotamian rulers.[15] But none of these rulers have any connection to Semiramis.

Semiramis, meanwhile, is not Babylonian at all — she is Assyrian, and not historical but legendary. The earliest references to Semiramis come from Greek sources nearly 1,500 years after Nimrod, such as Herodotus of Halicarnassus (*Histories 1.184 and 3.155)* and Ctesias of Cnidus (retold by Diodorus of Sicily, *World History 2.4-20* in 5th century BC).[16] They depict her as the wife of King Ninus — a fictional king invented in Greek literature, not an actual figure found in Assyrian king lists. There is no ancient record — none — placing

---

14. Ibid, Kindle ed., Loc. 2481

15. John M'Clintock and James Strong, "Nim'rod," in *Cyclopædia of Biblical, Theological, and Ecclesiastical Literature* (New York: Harper & Brothers, Publishers, 1894), 108.

16. Jona Lendering, "Semiramis," *Livius.org*, accessed November 15, 2024, https://www.livius.org/articles/mythology/semiramis/

Nimrod and Semiramis anywhere near each other in history. Hislop merges them by force, not by evidence.

Hislop's system begins to unravel the moment you examine the characters he tries to merge. One of his boldest moves is calling Semiramis the "Queen of Heaven," as though she were the Babylonian counterpart to Mary. But in the ancient world, that title belonged exclusively to Ishtar — a goddess, not a woman, and certainly not an Assyrian queen. There is no ancient inscription, no cuneiform tablet, no mythological text where Semiramis is ever called the "Queen of Heaven." Hislop only fuses them because their roles sound similar to him. It's the same method that makes him think every goddess is secretly the same woman and every god is secretly Nimrod in a Halloween costume. It isn't scholarship; it's theological connect-the-dots with no dots.

The problems only multiply when we turn to Tammuz. In actual Mesopotamian theology, Tammuz (Dumuzi) is never portrayed as the child of either Semiramis or Nimrod. He is the shepherd consort of Inanna/Ishtar, not their son. His entire myth cycle revolves around his marriage, death, and seasonal descent into the underworld. Nothing—absolutely nothing—in ancient Near Eastern literature describes him as the son of a deified king and queen. Hislop needs a mother-and-child pair to support his argument, so he simply invents one. He rewrites Tammuz's story, recasts Ishtar's role, and merges completely unrelated figures to make a point that the actual ancient sources contradict.

What makes Hislop's theory completely impossible is his timeline. For Hislop's trinity to be real, Nimrod would have to live a thousand years before Semiramis, marry her in the eighth century, and then father a child—Tammuz—who existed a thousand years before both of them. This is the chronological equivalent of claiming George

DEBUNKING THE PAGAN ROOTS OF CHRISTMAS

Washington married Cleopatra and they gave birth to Hercules. It is historically incoherent, archaeologically impossible, and linguistically indefensible. You cannot build history by ignoring history.

And that leads to the final, fatal blow: no ancient culture ever told the story Hislop claims existed. There is no "Babylonian holy family." No Nimrod–Semiramis marriage. No Tammuz-as-their-son. No winter-solstice birth. No December 25 festival. No ritual evergreen trees. Not in Babylonian literature. Not in Assyrian inscriptions. Not in Sumerian myths. Not in archaeology. Not in ancient commentary. Hislop's "trinity" is not found in the ancient world; it is found only in Victorian imagination. The moment you examine the primary sources, Hislop's entire construction collapses like a stage prop built out of tissue paper.

To dismantle Hislop is not to attack a scholar — it is to expose a system built on assumptions instead of evidence. When modern skeptics or Christians repeat Hislop's ideas, they are unknowingly spreading a nineteenth-century construction, not ancient Near Eastern history. The "Nimrod–Semiramis–Tammuz trinity" does not come from archaeology, linguistics, mythology, or Scripture. It comes from Hislop's imagination.

8

UNMASKING SANTA

THE SAINT BEHIND THE SUIT

Every December, the internet dusts off the same tired accusation: "Santa Claus is pagan!" Some claim he's a rebranded Norse god, others say he's tied to ancient shamans (an individual who acts as a bridge between the natural and supernatural worlds), and a few insist he's the winter cousin of Nimrod's imaginary family tree. But like most myths that go viral, these claims fall apart the moment you step into the real history. Because behind the red suit, the sleigh, and the marketing machine is not a pagan deity — it's a Christian bishop.

Before Santa became a brand, he was Nicholas of Myra — a fourth-century follower of Jesus known for his generosity, pastoral care, and his fierce defense of Christian doctrine.[1] This is the man who rescued the poor, protected the vulnerable, prayed for the sick, and possibly — depending on how spicy you like your church history — slapped Arius at the Council of Nicaea. He didn't ride a sleigh, but he did carry the gospel. He didn't live at the North Pole, but he did serve a coastal city in what is now Turkey. And he didn't climb down

---

1. Gulevich, *Encyclopedia of Christmas*, 521.

DEBUNKING THE PAGAN ROOTS OF CHRISTMAS 125

chimneys, but he did quietly drop money into the homes of struggling families at night.

The story of Santa Claus doesn't begin in a pagan temple or a Babylonian legend. It begins in the church — in a community shaped by Scripture, service, and sacrificial love. Somewhere along the way, the world swapped the bishop's miter for a red hat, the cross for a candy cane, and the message for marketing. But the roots remain. The Santa in the mall may be a symbol of holiday cheer, but the man behind the suit was a symbol of Christian compassion.

This chapter steps behind the costume and into the real story — the history that predates the myths, the facts that outlast the internet rumors, and the legacy of a man whose faith left a mark far deeper than the commercial character we've made him. Santa may sell the season, but Nicholas served the Savior.

The Pastor From Myra

Long before the North Pole ever entered the chat, Nicholas was born in the third century in Patara, a coastal city in what is now modern-day Turkey. He grew up in a wealthy Christian home, but wealth didn't grip his heart — Christ did. After his parents died, Nicholas inherited a great sum and did something completely countercultural: he gave it away. He didn't build a monument. He didn't buy political influence. He didn't establish a dynasty. He quietly blessed people in need.[2]

One of the most famous stories — attested early and preserved in multiple traditions — is about a poor father with three daughters. In

---

2. John M'Clintock and James Strong, "Nicholas (St.) of Myra," in *Cyclopædia of Biblical, Theological, and Ecclesiastical Literature* (New York: Harper & Brothers, Publishers, 1894), 61.

that culture, daughters without dowries faced a dark future. Nicholas heard of their plight and, under the cover of night, dropped bags of gold through their window so each daughter could marry with dignity.[3][4] He didn't wait to be thanked; he didn't leave a calling card. His ministry wasn't about being seen — it was about being faithful. Modern Santa slides down chimneys; Nicholas slid blessings into homes. Same generosity — very different story.

A Defender of the Faith, Not a Christmas Mascot

Nicholas eventually became Bishop of Myra, ministering during a time when confessing Christ could cost you your life. Under Diocletian's persecution, Nicholas was imprisoned for refusing to compromise his faith.[5] And when the persecution lifted, he didn't retreat — he stepped into the theological battles of the early church.

Tradition holds that Nicholas attended the Council of Nicaea in AD 325, where the divinity of Christ was under attack by Arius. This is supported by Nicholas' inclusion by Theodore the Lector in his list in *Historia Tripartita*, dated around AD 515.[6] Dr. Joshua Schachterle, who holds a Ph.D. in New Testament and Early Christianity, explains that that there are different lists of the attendees of the council which differ in the names they include or exclude. He notes

---

3. William J. Federer, *There Really Is a Santa Claus - History of Saint Nicholas & Christmas Holiday Traditions* (Amerisearch, 2002), 15.

4. Gulevich, *Encyclopedia of Christmas*, 523.

5. Federer, *There Really Is A Santa Claus*, 33.

6. St. Nicholas Center, "Bishop Nicholas Loses His Cool," accessed November 16, 2024, https://www.stnicholascenter.org/who-is-st-nicholas/stories-legends/traditional-stories/life-of-nicholas/bishop-nicholas-loses-his-cool

DEBUNKING THE PAGAN ROOTS OF CHRISTMAS   127

that "Nicholas of Myra" does appear on all the longest lists, including the one by Theodore, which is considered by scholars to be one of the more accurate, but not on the shorter.[7] The fact that he is not included on some lists may simply mean that Nicholas wasn't one of the more influential participants at the council.[8] Some accounts (and a lot of Christian memes) say Nicholas slapped Arius across the face for denying the deity of Jesus.[9] Whether or not the slap is literal, the legacy is clear: Nicholas stood unapologetically for orthodoxy. He defended the faith long before he ever became a Christmas symbol. Santa didn't start at the mall. He started a council defending Christ.

How St. Nicholas Became Santa Claus

After Nicholas died on December 6, 343 AD, his reputation spread across the Christian world.[10] Stories of his generosity, devotion to Christ, and miraculous interventions made him one of the most beloved saints in history. Churches were named after him from Rome to Russia. Sailors claimed him as their patron. Children learned to imitate his generosity. So how did a bishop from Turkey become a jolly gift-giver in a red suit? It didn't happen overnight — it unfolded in stages.

In Europe, "St. Nicholas" became "Sinterklaas." Dutch Christians celebrated Nicholas's feast day (December 6) with gift-giving, em-

---

7. Joshua Schachterle, "Did St. Nicholas Actually Attend the Council of Nicaea?," *Bart D. Ehrman Blog*, December 12, 2023, https://www.bartehrman.com/did-st-nicholas-actually-attend-the-council-of-nicaea/

8. Joshua Schachterle, "Did St. Nicholas Actually Attend the Council of Nicaea?"

9. St. Nicholas Center, "Bishop Nicholas Loses His Cool"

10. Federer, *There Really Is A Santa Claus*, 61.

phasizing his generosity to the poor. In Austria, the Netherlands, Belgium, Czechoslovakia, and parts of Germany, folk tradition cast St. Nicholas in the role of a Christmas season gift-bringer.[11] He was portrayed as an elderly, white-bearded man carrying a bishop's staff and dressed in a red bishop's robe and miter (ceremonial headgear worn by bishops and high-ranking clergy).[12] When Dutch settlers came to America, they brought Sinterklaas with them.[13] In America, "Sinterklaas" gradually transformed into "Santa Claus."

St. Nicholas and Secret Gift Giving

In these European countries, St. Nicholas was said to distribute presents in honor of his feast day. On the night of December 5, he would bring fruit, nuts, cookies, candy, and other small gifts to well-behaved children. Those who misbehaved too often might receive a stick as a warning. Children began to expect presents on St. Nicholas' Eve and started leaving containers where he could place the gifts.[14]

In Czechoslovakia, children attracted Nicholas by hanging stockings on the window frame.[15] In France, Saint Nicholas came to be associated with "Père Noël." Children would leave their slippers and wooden shoes on their doorsteps filled with oats to feed the camels of the three wise men and the next morning they discovered their

---

11. Gulevich, *Encyclopedia of Christmas*, 527.

12. Federer, *There Really Is A Santa Claus*, 87.

13. Ibid, 527.

14. Gulevich, *Encyclopedia of Christmas*, 528.

15. Ibid, 528.

DEBUNKING THE PAGAN ROOTS OF CHRISTMAS 129

kindness rewarded as their shoes were filled with sugared plums.[16] Germany, Italy, Belgium, Finland, Sweden, Norway, and other countries all had different names for Nicholas and varying traditions.[17]

Researchers believe this custom of giving gifts to children on St. Nicholas' Day started in the twelfth century. The Reformation in 1517 shifted the focus from praying or honoring specific saints, including Nicholas, believing that Christ alone should be the focus.[18] People still enjoyed the gift-giving, so in the centuries that followed, the Christkindel (pronounced "Kris Kindl" and later "Kris Kingle" in old German) became the Christmas season gift-bringer in much of Germany.

Washington Irving first introduced St. Nicholas to American literature in 1809, depicting him as a gift-bearing figure in *A History of New York*.[19] Clement Clarke Moore's 1823 poem "A Visit from St. Nicholas" standardized the sleigh, reindeer, chimney descent, and cheerful Christmas spirit.[20] But it was Thomas Nast's nineteenth-century illustrations in *Harper's Weekly*—beginning in 1863—that fixed Santa's physical appearance, giving him the red suit, round belly, North Pole home, and workshop that Americans recognize today.[21]

---

16. Federer, *There Really Is A Santa Claus*, 85.

17. Ibid, 85.

18. Federer, *There Really Is A Santa Claus*, 101.

19. Washington Irving, *A History of New York*, by Diedrich Knickerbocker (New York: Inskeep & Bradford, 1809).

20. Clement Clarke Moore, "A Visit from St. Nicholas," *Troy Sentinel* (December 23, 1823).

21. Thomas Nast, "Santa Claus in Camp," *Harper's Weekly*, January 3, 1863.

Is Santa Inspired by Odin?

One of the trendiest modern claims is that Christmas customs — especially Santa Claus, reindeer, and gift-giving — originated from the Norse god Odin. It's a popular internet theory because it "feels" ancient and mysterious, but the historical receipts say otherwise. Odin is a late figure in Germanic mythology whose stories were recorded primarily between the eleventh and thirteenth centuries in texts like the *Prose Edda* and *Poetic Edda*. By the time these sources were written, Christianity had already spread across Northern Europe for centuries. Odin's myths were preserved *after* Christianization, not before, which means they cannot be the source of Christian customs that existed long before these texts were penned. In fact, nothing in the earliest Christian celebrations of Christmas (2nd–5th centuries AD) shows any engagement with Norse gods — which makes sense, because Odin worship never touched the Mediterranean world where Christmas developed.

In descriptions of Odin's appearance — such as those found in *The Saga of the Volsungs* — he doesn't wear red; he wears blue, gray, or spotted clothing.[22] The idea that Santa is a rebranded Odin usually comes from three supposed parallels: Odin's eight-legged horse Sleipnir, the "Wild Hunt," and Odin's long white beard. But none of these hold up.

---

22. Eiríkr Magnússon et al., *The Völsunga Saga*, trans. William Morris and Jessie L. Weston (London & New York: Norrœna Society, 1907), 216. Accessed November 16, 2025, https://archive.org/details/volsungasaga00eir

Sleipnir was an eight-legged horse, not a reindeer. Odin rode Sleipnir directly; he did not travel in a sleigh.[23] The "Wild Hunt" — whether called Oskoreia or Åsgårdsrei — is a medieval ghost procession, not a pagan precursor to Santa's midnight travels. And Odin giving "gifts" usually meant arming warriors for battle, not blessing children with joy and candy. As Dr. Jackson Crawford explains, Odin and the Wild Hunt "represent the terror of winter," not generosity.. Santa Claus represents the generosity of spirit that we certainly hope that we receive whatever holiday we celebrate. Odin also wasn't bringing gifts to children, he gives gifts to men he is directly going to directly harvest (kill) for his army. Odin wasn't bringing gifts to children; he was recruiting warriors for Ragnarok.[24]

Odin's most famous intervention and gift-giving in the saga occurs in Chapter III: "Of the Sword that Sigmund, Volsung's son, drew from the Branstock" where Odin, in disguise, thrusts a sword into the trunk of an oak tree, *Barnstokkr*, and declares that the man who can remove the sword from the tree will receive a gift and never carry a better weapon. All the guests fail, but Sigmund, the young son of King Völsung, effortlessly pulls the sword free.[25] The whole challenge serves the purpose of assessing the worthiness of individuals and to shape the destiny of the Völsung lineage, ensuring they live and die as glorious warriors. Odin's gifts to men were restricted to swords and war-gear

---

23. Spencer McDaniel, "The Long, Strange, Fascinating History of Santa Claus," *Tales of Times Forgotten*, December 7, 2019, https://talesoftimesforgotten.com/2019/12/07/the-long-strange-fascinating-history-of-santa-claus/

24. Jackson Crawford, *Odin Isn't Santa Claus*, YouTube video, 3:28, November 25, 2020, https://youtu.be/_o5ih9WuCxQ?si=L-FDE1Mst-8rnAwZ

25. Magnússon, *The Völsunga Saga*, 37.

for his own warriors, and he came to spread mischief abroad rather than goodwill or even good luck.[26]

Aside from their shared long beards, the symbols and appearance associated with Odin and Santa Claus are completely different. Old Norse stories often describe Odin as a grim, elderly man who has only one eye and a long, gray beard. We know the beard is gray because some texts, such as verses in the poems *Grímnismál* and *Óðins nöfn*, call him "Hárbarðr," which literally translates to "Graybeard."[27]

In short: Odin didn't fly, didn't bring gifts, didn't ride a sleigh, and had nothing to do with Nicholas of Myra. The claim that Christmas came from Norse paganism isn't history — it's a modern remix built on assumptions, not evidence. Christmas customs developed in Christian culture, not in the halls of Valhalla.

A Final Word: History Is Not a Mandate

Now that we've unmasked Santa and traced the story back to its real source, it's important to be crystal clear about what this chapter does and does not prove. Showing that Santa Claus ultimately traces back to St. Nicholas of Myra — a Christian bishop known for generosity and orthodox conviction — does not mean Christians are required to participate in Christmas traditions. It doesn't make Santa "biblical," and it doesn't place Christmas on the same level as the commands

---

26. Hilda R. Davis, "Scandinavian Folklore in Britain," *Journal of the Folklore Institute* 7, no. 2/3 (Aug.–Dec. 1970): 177-86.

27. Spencer McDaniel, "No, Santa Is Not Inspired by Odin," *Tales of Times Forgotten*, December 27, 2021, https://talesoftimesforgotten.com/2021/12/27/no-santa-claus-is-not-inspired-by-odin/

of Scripture. History can inform us, correct us, and free us from misinformation — but history does not create obligations.

We can have the intellectual honesty to say this plainly: St. Nicholas' story is honorable, but that doesn't make the modern Santa Claus tradition a divine command. It simply means that the origin of the tradition is Christian — not pagan, not Babylonian, not Norse, not shamanic, and not occult. It means the story was born in the soil of generosity, not idolatry. But that's where the requirement ends. The commercialization of his image in the modern world is real, and the red suit today has far more to do with advertising than with ancient liturgy. The kindness Nicholas embodied can inspire us, but it cannot bind us.

Some believers choose to give gifts at Christmas in honor of the gifts given to Christ. Others give as a reminder of the gift Christ gave to us — salvation, grace, and undeserved mercy. Others choose not to participate at all, whether out of preference, conscience, or simplicity. That freedom is Christian liberty, and the New Testament upholds it (Rom. 14:5–6; Col. 2:16–17). You are not more holy if you celebrate Christmas, and you are not more faithful if you do not. What matters is that whatever you do, you do unto the Lord with a clear conscience.

But what we cannot do — not honestly — is call Santa or Christmas "pagan" when the evidence says otherwise. Too much history refutes that claim. Too many ancient sources contradict it. Too many modern myths have been repeatedly debunked. And the documented life of Nicholas of Myra stands as a quiet rebuke to every internet rumor that tries to drag a faithful Christian bishop into a pagan origin he never had.

So as we close this chapter, remember the purpose of this book: we aren't trying to force Christmas on anyone. We aren't trying to baptize consumerism. We aren't trying to make Santa a theological mandate.

We are simply putting truth back on the table. Santa's roots are Christian. Christmas is not pagan. And what you choose to do with that truth — in freedom, conscience, and conviction — is between you and the Lord.

9

THE TRUE ROOTS OF THE CHRISTMAS TREE

CHOPPING DOWN THE LIES

Every Christmas, the same rumor gets dragged out of storage like a dusty ornament nobody even likes: "The Christmas tree is pagan!" And every year, Christians find themselves on defense against conspiracy theories that have more branches than truth. Let's get this out of the way early—the only thing getting "chopped down" in this chapter are the lies.

For centuries, people have claimed the Christmas tree came from druids worshiping forests, Vikings bowing to Yggdrasil, or Babylonians building shrines to Nimrod. The problem? Not a single one of those theories stands up once you put real history, real dates, and real sources to it. What you're going to see in this chapter is simple: the Christmas tree doesn't grow out of pagan soil—it grows out of Christian witness.

From Tertullian calling believers "evergreen" in the 200s, to St. Boniface literally knocking down a pagan oak to preach Christ, to medieval Christians using "paradise trees" to teach Genesis, to Martin Luther pointing to the Light of the World with candles on an evergreen, the Christmas tree has been a symbol of Christ, not of paganism.

This is what happens when Christians don't copy the world—they confront it, correct it, and convert entire cultures with the gospel. This is what happens when the Light steps into darkness. This is what happens when truth stands taller than myth. So grab your axe—metaphorically—and let's start chopping, because the true roots of the Christmas tree don't point to ancient idolatry. They point to Jesus.

Witness Of Tertullian

One of the earliest hints of evergreen symbolism tied to the Christian faith shows up not in pagan mythology but in the writings of Tertullian around the year 200. He described believers as "a tree ever green"—a picture of a life rooted in Christ that doesn't wither when the seasons change.[1] Long before anyone strung lights, hung ornaments, or created an entire seasonal aisle at Target, Christians were already using tree imagery to proclaim the gospel. For Tertullian, the evergreen symbolized the steadfast, unchanging, ever-living nature of a disciple whose hope is anchored in Christ. This wasn't syncretism. It was theology. Christians didn't borrow from pagans; they drew from Scripture's own rich botanical imagery.

St. Boniface and The Oak That Couldn't Stand Against the Cross

---

1. Tertullian, On Idolatry, chap. 15, in The Ante-Nicene Fathers, vol. 3, ed. Alexander Roberts and James Donaldson (Buffalo, NY: Christian Literature Publishing Co., 1885), accessed November 16, 2024, https://www.newadvent.org/fathers/0302.htm

DEBUNKING THE PAGAN ROOTS OF CHRISTMAS 137

Fast forward a few centuries, and things get a lot more dramatic. In the early 700s, a missionary named St. Boniface was sent to preach the gospel to pagan tribes in what is now Germany. When he arrived in the region of Geismar, he encountered a horrifying ritual — locals were preparing to offer a young boy as a sacrifice to their god Thor at the base of a massive oak known as the *Donar* or *Jupiter Oak*. Boniface stepped forward and declared that the sacrifice would not happen. With boldness only the Holy Spirit could supply, he took up an axe and began cutting into the "sacred" tree. Before he could finish, a violent wind ripped the oak from its roots and sent it crashing to the ground. The stunned pagans immediately recognized that Thor had failed to defend his own tree, and many of them turned to Christ.[2]

Behind the fallen oak stood a small, untouched fir tree stretching its green branches toward heaven. Boniface pointed to it and told the people that this tree—not the blood-stained oak—would represent the peace, eternal life, and heavenly hope found in Christ.[3] Here we have the earliest clear connection between Christian mission, the message of the gospel, and the use of an evergreen as a symbol of Christ's life. This was not Christians adopting a pagan practice; it was Christians overturning one. It wasn't syncretism—it was spiritual warfare. The gospel didn't bow to the culture. The gospel confronted the culture, flipped the script, and converted an entire people.

When the Lights Come On, the Lies Turn Off

---

[2]. Federer, *There Really Is A Santa Claus*, 164-165.

[3]. Henry van Dyke, "The Oak of Geismar," *Scribner's Magazine* 10 (July–December 1891): 686.

The roots of the Christmas tree go even deeper into Judeo-Christian tradition through the symbolism of light. Long before LED bulbs or twinkling string lights wrapped around evergreens, the Jewish people celebrated the Festival of Lights—Hanukkah. This annual feast commemorated the rededication of the temple after Antiochus Epiphanes desecrated it with idol worship. When the temple was purified, the menorah was relit with only enough oil for one day. In a miracle recorded in Jewish tradition, the oil lasted eight days until new oil could be prepared.[4] Light, therefore, became a symbol of God's presence, purity, and power over darkness. So when Christians later placed lights on trees, they weren't borrowing from pagans. They were drawing from the heritage of God's people and proclaiming what Jesus Himself said: "I am the light of the world."

One of the most beloved legends surrounding the Christmas tree involves Martin Luther in the early 1500s. One cold Christmas Eve, Luther was walking home under a sky filled with bright winter stars. The beauty overwhelmed him, and when he returned home, he set up a small evergreen tree, placing candles on its branches so his children could visualize the glory he had just witnessed—the heavens declaring the birth of Christ.[5] Whether this story is perfectly historical or somewhat embellished, what matters is the meaning Christians attached to the practice: the tree symbolized heaven touching earth, and the lights represented the radiance of Christ entering our darkness.

Paradise Trees: The Gospel in Branches

---

4. Federer, *There Really Is A Santa Claus*, 164.

5. Ibid, 164-165.

But the clearest bridge between medieval Christianity and the modern Christmas tree is found in the Paradise Plays. During the Middle Ages, the church used dramatic performances to teach Scripture to a largely illiterate population. One of the most popular plays—performed on December 24—told the story of Adam and Eve's fall.[6] At the center of the stage stood a "Paradise Tree," usually an evergreen, decorated with apples to represent the forbidden fruit and white wafers to symbolize Christ's redemption.[7] When these plays were banned in the 1500s due to rowdy behavior, families began bringing the Paradise Tree tradition into their homes. Over time, the apples evolved into ornaments, the wafers into baked goods, and the tree itself became a staple of Christmas celebrations. This is the earliest direct ancestor of the Christmas tree as we know it.

As Christmas traditions continued to develop, German Christian culture played a major role in shaping what we recognize today. Children exchanged apples and food gifts at Christmastime as early as the tenth century. With the rise of St. Nicholas traditions — originally tied to December 6 — gift-giving eventually shifted to Christmas Day. Guilds, churches, and families all incorporated decorated evergreens into their celebration of the Nativity. As time went on, ornaments became more elaborate, candles gave way to safer lighting, and the Christmas tree spread throughout Europe and eventually into American life. At every stage, the meaning remained consistent: the evergreen pointed to eternal life, the lights to Christ's radiance, the ornaments to God's blessings, and the gifts to God's ultimate gift—His Son.

---

6. Brunner, Bernd. *Inventing the Christmas Tree*. Translated by Benjamin A. Smith. Yale University Press, 2017, 15. https://doi.org/10.12987/9780300188868.

7. Bernd Brunner, *Inventing the Christmas Tree*, 15.

When you trace the story honestly, you see something beautiful: Christians weren't copying pagans—they were catechizing their children. Every symbol attached to the Christmas tree proclaims the gospel: The evergreen whispers of life that never fades. The lights declare that darkness has been defeated. The ornaments recall the blessings and fruit of redemption. The gifts reflect the generosity of the God who gave us Christ.

The Christmas tree doesn't point to Thor. It doesn't point to Odin. It doesn't point to Nimrod. It points upward—to the Savior who hung on a tree for our salvation, rose again in triumph, and offers eternal life to all who believe. Christians didn't borrow the Christmas tree from paganism. Christians reclaimed the world God created and reoriented it toward its rightful King. This is what happens when the Light enters the world. This is what happens when truth stands taller than myth. This is what happens when the gospel transforms cultures and remakes symbols. The real roots of the Christmas tree don't run into pagan soil—they run straight to Christ.

Axes, Idols, and Bad Exegesis: What Jeremiah 10 Actually Says

Every December, the same claim reappears like an unwanted regift: "Jeremiah 10 condemns Christmas trees." And every December, it becomes clear that the loudest people in the debate have never once read Jeremiah in context. To handle this passage faithfully, we must start with exegesis, which simply means reading the Bible the way the author intended—within its historical, cultural, and literary setting. The opposite is eisegesis, which is when someone drags their own ideas, opinions, memes, or TikTok theology *into* the text and forces it to say something it never said. Jeremiah 10 only becomes a "Christmas

DEBUNKING THE PAGAN ROOTS OF CHRISTMAS 141

tree passage" when someone does eisegesis. But when we put Jeremiah back in his world, the myth collapses instantly.

Jeremiah ministered to both the Northern and Southern Kingdoms of Israel during a politically unstable and spiritually rebellious period. Ten tribes had already been exiled by Assyria in 722 BC, and Judah itself was now sliding toward judgment. His message in chapters 7–10 formed one unified sermon calling out Judah's hypocrisy in worship. Jeremiah preached from roughly 627 to 586 BC—from the looming threats of Assyria and Egypt to the rise of Babylon, who would ultimately destroy Jerusalem. His purpose was urgent and clear: Judah had fallen under the curse of God because of persistent idolatry, and unless they repented, exile was certain. Simply put, Jeremiah was not warning the people about holiday traditions. He was warning a nation on the brink of destruction about worshiping false gods.

This is where many modern readers miss the point: the Bible is filled with trees—beautiful, symbolic, God-glorifying trees. Scripture speaks of cedars that the Lord planted (Ps 104:16), of trees clapping their hands as they rejoice before God (Isa 55:12–13), and of cypress and pine used to beautify God's sanctuary (Isa 60:13). So whatever Jeremiah 10 is talking about, it is not condemning the existence or decorative use of trees. God Himself uses trees as symbols of blessing, life, and worship.

When we finally turn to Jeremiah 10, the context is unmistakable. Judah was surrounded by cultures obsessed with astral deities—sun, moon, star, and planetary gods believed to control fate and reveal omens.[8] People feared eclipses, comets, and unusual celestial events,

---

8. Elmer A. Martens, "Jeremiah," in Evangelical Commentary on the Bible, vol. 3, Baker Reference Library (Grand Rapids, MI: Baker Book House, 1995), 529.

believing these were messages from the gods.[9] Jeremiah warns Judah not to learn these superstitions or imitate the religious practices of the nations. He draws a sharp contrast between handmade idols and the living God. As one scholar put it, Jeremiah alternates between mocking idols and praising God to highlight the absurdity of their idolatry—idols in verses 3–5, God in 6–7, idols again in 8–9, God in 10, idols in 11, God in 12–13, idols in 14–15, and finally God again in verse 16.[10] Jeremiah's purpose is not seasonal; it is theological warfare.

Jeremiah vividly describes how idols were made in the ancient world. A craftsman cut down a tree, shaped the wood, overlaid it with silver and gold plating, and then fastened the statue upright so it wouldn't topple over. "With cutting sarcasm the process of shaping, stabilizing, and clothing these gods is described... the idols are nonfunctioning, a work of errors, and an embarrassment to their makers".[11] The issue has nothing to do with an evergreen in a home; it has everything to do with a carved wooden image dressed up like a deity and worshiped as a real god.

Another scholar notes that Jeremiah's audience had been tempted by the magnificent idols of Babylon. Some Israelites, already in exile or soon to be, were impressed by Babylonian temples, celestial gods, and astrological signs.[12] Jeremiah responds by ridiculing the idols themselves, asking how people could worship "a piece of wood"

---

9. F. B. Huey, Jeremiah, Lamentations, vol. 16, The New American Commentary (Nashville: Broadman & Holman Publishers, 1993), 125.

10. Martens, *Jeremiah*, 529.

11. Martens, *Jeremiah*, 529.

12. Victor Harold Matthews, Mark W. Chavalas, and John H. Walton, The IVP Bible Background Commentary: Old Testament, electronic ed. (Downers Grove, IL: InterVarsity Press, 2000), Je 10:2.

DEBUNKING THE PAGAN ROOTS OF CHRISTMAS 143

decorated with gold and silver plating and secured with nails so it wouldn't fall. He mocks the wooden idol as "a scarecrow in a melon patch (v.5)," unable to speak, move, or act.[13] The point is simple: idols made by human hands have no power. They cannot move unless carried, cannot speak unless imagined, and cannot save because they are lifeless.

Jeremiah's critique cuts even deeper. In verses 1–16, he shows that idols are lifeless products crafted by humans, while God is the living Creator of heaven and earth. Idols have not created anything; they inspire fear because of superstition, not because they have any actual power. In contrast, God alone made the heavens, controls the weather, governs creation, and rules the nations. Idolatry is not merely foolish—it is rebellion against the One true God. As another commentary notes, Jeremiah highlights the "nonsense of bowing down to what merchants have imported and craftsmen have made."[14] Worshiping an artifact instead of the Maker of all things is the heart of Israel's sin.

Once we see the actual context, the myth evaporates. Jeremiah 10 is not addressing seasonal decoration, winter festivals, or evergreen trees placed in a home. Jeremiah is attacking the idolatry of carving a wooden image, plating it with precious metals, stabilizing it so it won't tip over, and bowing to it in fear. He is mocking the impotence of false gods worshiped by the nations. He is confronting people tempted by Babylonian religion. He is exposing the foolishness of a culture terrified by omens and infatuated with celestial idols. This has nothing

---

13. Huey, *Jeremiah, Lamentations*, 125.

14. J. Gordon McConville, "Jeremiah," in New Bible Commentary: 21st Century Edition, ed. D. A. Carson et al., 4th ed. (Leicester, England; Downers Grove, IL: Inter-Varsity Press, 1994), 682.

to do with Christmas and everything to do with the spiritual adultery of Israel.

The Christmas tree is not an idol carved, plated, worshiped, carried in procession, or feared as a god. It is a symbol of joy, a cultural tradition, and for many believers, a reminder of the Light of the World who entered the darkness. To claim Jeremiah 10 condemns Christmas trees is to rip the text out of its historical context and commit the very error we warned against: eisegesis. Jeremiah was not preaching against Christmas. He was preaching against idols. Not a single ancient source — Hebrew, Babylonian, Roman, or Norse — ever describes the Christmas tree as a pagan object.

10

LIBERTY, NOT LEGALISM: WHY CELEBRATING CHRISTMAS ISN'T SIN

AND WHY NO ONE CAN CALL IT PAGAN

Every year, arguments about Christmas break out across social media timelines like clockwork. Some claim Christians shouldn't celebrate Christmas because "God never commanded it." Others say observing Christmas is sinful because only the feasts in Leviticus 23 are "biblically authorized." And still others argue that celebrating Jesus' birth (or any holiday not named in Scripture) is somehow equivalent to paganism. These claims may sound spiritual — but they crumble under the weight of the Bible itself.

From beginning to end, Scripture gives us a better, wiser, more balanced framework. The Bible never commands believers to celebrate Christmas — but it also never forbids it. And more importantly, the Bible shows us something the critics never mention: Jesus Himself participated in celebrations that God never commanded. That one fact alone dismantles the entire "If God didn't command it, you can't celebrate it" argument. But that's only the beginning.

Let's walk through the biblical evidence, the historical context, and the theological principles that lead us to one simple conclusion: Christmas is not pagan — and Christians have full liberty in Christ to celebrate it or not celebrate it, so long as they do all things to the glory of God.

The Bible Is Filled With People Who Celebrated the Birth of Christ

Before we say anything else, let's make one thing abundantly clear: the Bible itself shows angels, shepherds, prophets, and wise men celebrating the birth and incarnation of Jesus. The heavenly host erupted in praise (Luke 2:13). Shepherds returned "glorifying and praising God" (Luke 2:20). Simeon lifted the infant Christ and blessed God (Luke 2:28). Anna proclaimed the Messiah to everyone around her (Luke 2:38). The Magi traveled far, bowed before the child, and offered gifts (Matt. 2:11). If heaven celebrated the birth of Christ, Christians certainly may.

Critics often ask, "Where did God command us to celebrate Christ's birth?" But that is the wrong question. The real question is: Where did God forbid it? The birth of Christ is the turning point of human history — the moment when God became flesh and dwelt among us for our redemption. Celebrating that is not sin. It is worship.

Feasts, Fulfillment, and Freedom: The New Covenant View of Leviticus 23

One of the most persistent claims made by critics of Christmas is that Christians are only permitted to observe the feasts prescribed by God in Leviticus 23. The argument sounds biblical on the surface, but it collapses as soon as you read the New Testament. The feasts of Leviticus 23 were given to Israel under the Old Covenant, not to the Church under the New Covenant. They were covenant markers for a specific people, in a specific land, under a specific law. And Scripture itself tells us that every one of those feasts pointed beyond themselves to something greater than Israel's yearly calendar: they pointed to Christ.

The feasts were never meant to be permanent obligations for all peoples everywhere. They were prophetic shadows cast by the coming Messiah. Paul makes this explicit when he writes, "These are a shadow of what was to come; the substance is Christ" (Col. 2:16–17). Shadows don't bind the conscience once the substance arrives. The feasts were rehearsals; Christ is the main event. And when the apostles were confronted with the question of whether Gentile Christians needed to keep Jewish feasts or the Sabbath, their answer—guided by the Holy Spirit—was an emphatic no. The Jerusalem Council placed no such burden on Gentile believers (Acts 15:28–29). No feasts. No Sabbaths. No Levitical calendar. The new covenant does not place Christians under the old covenant's festival obligations.

This makes perfect sense once we understand the prophetic design of the feasts themselves. The feasts of Leviticus 23 were not miscellaneous holidays; they were divine signposts pointing toward the person and work of Jesus Christ.

Passover foreshadowed the sacrificial death of Jesus, the true Lamb of God whose blood delivers us from judgment. The Feast of Unleavened Bread reflected His sinless life and burial, the One without leaven resting in the tomb. Firstfruits anticipated His resurrection as "the firstfruits of those who have fallen asleep" (1 Cor. 15:20). Pentecost found its fulfillment in the outpouring of the Holy Spirit in Acts 2, the first great harvest of redeemed humanity. These four feasts are fulfilled with breathtaking precision in Christ's first coming.

The final three feasts—Trumpets, Atonement, and Tabernacles—look forward to the completion of Christ's work. The Feast of Trumpets anticipates the return of the Lord with the sound of God's trumpet. The Day of Atonement points to Christ's once-for-all sacrifice, fully realized when Israel finally turns to Him in repentance. And the Feast of Tabernacles foresees the final dwelling of God with His people in the new creation. Taken together, the seven feasts form a prophetic calendar that spans Christ's death, burial, resurrection, Spirit-outpouring, return, judgment, and eternal kingdom. Once the substance has arrived, the shadows no longer function as binding requirements. Christ is the fulfillment.

That is why Paul warns believers not to let anyone judge them "in regard to a festival or a new moon or a Sabbath day" (Col. 2:16). Those who insist Christians *must* keep Leviticus 23 are binding consciences where God gives freedom and are elevating shadows above the One they were meant to reveal. The early Church understood this perfectly. The apostles did not command Gentiles to observe the feasts. The New Testament nowhere requires them. And Jesus Himself participated in celebrations—like Hanukkah and likely Purim—that were never commanded by God at all. The feasts were good. Christ is better. And in Him, believers enjoy freedom, not legalistic obligation.

But What About Birthdays?

Some critics point out that Jews historically did not celebrate birthdays. This is true — annual birthday parties were not part of Jewish tradition. But the Bible does record birthday celebrations (Gen 40:20; Matt 14:6; Mark 6:21), and more importantly, Judaism did mark milestones with celebration: weaning (Gen 21:8), bar/bat mitzvah,

DEBUNKING THE PAGAN ROOTS OF CHRISTMAS 149

age-specific achievements (Pirke Avot 5:21), and upsheren (first haircut at age 3).[1]

These were not "God-commanded feasts," yet they were honored. The problem with Pharaoh and Herod was not their birthdays — it was their evil. The celebration wasn't sinful. Their actions were. Birthdays were not commanded but were culturally acceptable, meaningful, and integrated into Jewish life. The same is true for Christmas.

Christian Liberty: The Final Word

The final authority on this entire debate comes straight from the apostle Paul:

"One person judges one day to be more important than another day; someone else judges every day to be the same. Let each one be fully convinced in his own mind. Whoever observes the day, observes it for the Lord" (Romans 14:5–6). Here is biblical wisdom at its finest: You can celebrate unto the Lord. You can abstain unto the Lord. But you may not judge another believer for either choice. This is the heart of Christian liberty. This is the balance of Scripture. This is the freedom of the gospel.

Christmas is not about the date. It is not about the calendar. It is not about December 25. It is not about Roman myths, pagan claims, or internet conspiracies. It is about the event — the incarnation. The miracle of God becoming man. The coming of the Redeemer. The hope of the nations arriving in human flesh. You are not obligated to

---

[1]. "Bar and Bat Mitzvah," *ReformJudaism.org*, accessed November 16, 2025, https://reformjudaism.org/beliefs-practices/lifecycle-rituals/religious-education-rituals/bar-and-bat-mitzvah.

celebrate Christmas. You are not obligated to put up a tree. You are not obligated to observe any tradition you do not desire to observe. But you *are* free to celebrate the birth of Christ with joy. You *are* free to gather with believers and family to honor the Savior. You *are* free to proclaim the good news with festive delight. What you are not free to do is call Christmas pagan when Scripture, history, and logic all refute that claim. And you are not free to bind the conscience of another believer where God Himself has given liberty.

In the end, Christmas is not a command — and not a compromise. It is not a requirement — and not a rebellion. It is not a pagan infiltration — and not a divine obligation. It is an option, a freedom, a celebration, and for millions of believers throughout history, a Christ-centered expression of worship. Those who celebrate may do so unto the Lord. Those who abstain may do so unto the Lord. But no one may condemn the other. Because Christmas was never about a date. It was always about a Savior. And celebrating the Savior is always biblical.

BIBLIOGRAPHY

"A Homily in Preparation for the Celebration of Christmas According to Saint John Chrysostom." *Orthodox Ethos*. Accessed November 16, 2025.https://www.orthodoxethos.com/post/a-homily-in-preparation-for-the-celebration-of-christmas-according-to-saint-john-chrysostom

A. C. Bhaktivedanta Swami Prabhupāda, trans. *Śrīmad-Bhāgavatam (Bhāgavata Purāṇa)*. Vedabase. Accessed November 12, 2025. https://vedabase.io/en/library/sb/.

Africanus, Julius. *Chronographiai*. Fragment in The Ante-Nicene Fathers, Vol. 6. Edited by Alexander Roberts and James Donaldson. Buffalo, NY: Christian Literature Publishing Co., 1886.

Anonymous. *On the Solstices and the Equinoxes of the Conception and Nativity of Our Lord Jesus Christ and of John the Baptist.* Translated by Isabella Image. Edited by Roger Pearse. 2022. https://www.roger-pearse.com/weblog/2022/02/05/de-solstitiis-et-aequinoctiis-cpl-2277-now-online-in-english/

Augustine. *On the Trinity.* In *Nicene and Post-Nicene Fathers*, First Series, Vol. 3. Edited by Philip Schaff. Buffalo, NY: Christian Literature Publishing Co., 1887. Accessed November 3, 2025. https ://www.newadvent.org/fathers/130104.htm.

Augustine. *Sermons for Christmas and Epiphany*. Translated by Thomas Comerford Lawler. Ancient Christian Writers, no. 15. Westminster, MD: Newman Press, 1952.

Babylonian Talmud. Rosh Hashanah 10b–11a.

"Bar and Bat Mitzvah." *ReformJudaism.org*. Accessed November 16, 2025.https://reformjudaism.org/beliefs-practices/lifecycle-ri tuals/religious-education-rituals/bar-and-bat-mitzvah

Barry, John D., David Bomar, Derek R. Brown, Rachel Klippenstein, Douglas Mangum, Carrie Sinclair Wolcott, Lazarus Wentz, Elliot Ritzema, and Wendy Widder, eds. *The Lexham Bible Dictionary*. Bellingham, WA: Lexham Press, 2016.

Bhaktivedanta Swami Prabhupāda, A. C., trans. *Śrīmad-Bhāgavatam (Bhāgavata Purāṇa)*. Vedabase. Accessed November 14, 2025. ht tps://vedabase.io/en/library/sb/10/1/34/.

Blomberg, Craig L. *The Historical Reliability of the Gospels*. Second Edition. Downers Grove, IL; Nottingham, England: IVP Academic: An Imprint of InterVarsity Press; Apollos, 2007.

Broocks, Rice, and Travis Thrasher. *Man, Myth, Messiah: Answering History's Greatest Question*. Nashville, TN: W Publishing Group, 2016.

Brunner, Bernd. *Inventing the Christmas Tree*. Translated by Benjamin A. Smith. Yale University Press, 2017. https://doi.org/10. 12987/9780300188868.

Butler, John G. *Analytical Bible Expositor: Matthew* (Clinton, IA: LBC Publications, 2008).

Cartwright, Mark. "Temple of Saturn, Roman Forum." *World History Encyclopedia*. Last modified April 26, 2012. https://www.wo rldhistory.org/image/2182/temple-of-saturn-roman-forum/.

Cole, Susan Guettel. "12. Voices from beyond the Grave: Dionysus and the Dead". *Masks of Dionysus*, edited by Thomas H. Carpenter and Christopher A. Faraone, Ithaca, NY: Cornell University Press, 1993, pp. 276-296. https://doi.org/10.7591/9781501733680-017

Clement of Alexandria. *The Stromata, or Miscellanies*. Vol. 2 of *The Ante-Nicene Fathers*. Edited by Alexander Roberts and James Donaldson. Buffalo, NY: Christian Literature Publishing Co., 1885.

Chrysostom, John. *Homily 2 on Christmas Day*. Translated by W. C. Cotterill. In *A Select Library of the Nicene and Post-Nicene Fathers of the Christian Church*, First Series, Vol. 14. Edited by Philip Schaff. New York: Charles Scribner's Sons, 1889. Accessed November 3, 2025. https://www.tertullian.org/fathers/chrysostom_homily_2_on_christmas.htm

Clayton, Matt. *Egyptian Gods: A Captivating Guide to Atum, Horus, Seth, Isis, Anubis, Ra, Thoth, Sekhmet, Geb, Hathor and Other Gods and Goddesses of Ancient Egypt*. Independently Published, 2020.

Crawford, Jackson. "Jackson Crawford – Norse Mythology: Real Expertise. No Agendas." Accessed November 16, 2025. https://jacksonwcrawford.com/

Crawford, Jackson. *Odin Isn't Santa Claus*. YouTube video, 11:44. November 25, 2020. https://youtu.be/_o5ih9WuCxQ?si=L-FDE1Mst-8rnAwZ.

Cross, F. L., and Elizabeth A. Livingstone, eds. *The Oxford Dictionary of the Christian Church*. Oxford; New York: Oxford University Press, 2005.

Davis, Hilda R. "Scandinavian Folklore in Britain." *Journal of the Folklore Institute* 7, no. 2/3 (Aug.–Dec. 1970): 177-86.

Dunand, Francoise, and Christiane Zivie-Coche. *Gods and Men in Egypt: 3000 BCE to 395 CE*. Translated by David Lorton. Ithaca, NY: Cornell University Press, 2005.

Dyer, Charles H. "Ezekiel." In *The Bible Knowledge Commentary: An Exposition of the Scriptures*, edited by J. F. Walvoord and R. B. Zuck. Wheaton, IL: Victor Books, 1985.

Euripides. *The Bacchae*. Translated by T. A. Buckley; revised by Alex Sens; further revised by Gregory Nagy. Accessed November 12, 2025. https://www.uh.edu/~cldue/texts/bacchae.html.

Federer, William J. *There Really Is a Santa Claus - History of Saint Nicholas & Christmas Holiday Traditions*. Amerisearch, 2002.

Froelich, Margaret. "Serapis." In *The Lexham Bible Dictionary*, edited by John D. Barry, David Bomar, Derek R. Brown, Rachel Klippenstein, Douglas Mangum, Carrie Sinclair Wolcott, Lazarus Wentz, Elliot Ritzema, and Wendy Widder. Bellingham, WA: Lexham Press, 2016.

Gay, Jerome. *The Whitewashing of Christianity: A Hidden Past, a Hurtful Present, and a Hopeful Future* (Chicago, IL: 13th & Joan, 2021).

Green, W. C., trans. *Egils Saga*. 1893. PDF. Icelandic Saga Database. Accessed November 11, 2025. https://sagadb.org/files/pdf/egils_saga.en.pdf.

Gulevich, Tanya. *Encyclopedia of Christmas*. Detroit, MI: Omnigraphics, 2003.

Elwell, Walter A., and Barry J. Beitzel. *Baker Encyclopedia of the Bible*. Grand Rapids, MI: Baker Book House, 1988.

Elwell, Walter A. and Beitzel, Barry J. "Calendars, Ancient and Modern," in *Baker Encyclopedia of the Bible* (Grand Rapids, MI: Baker Book House, 1988).

Elwell, Walter A. and Beitzel, Barry J., in *Baker Encyclopedia of the Bible* (Grand Rapids, MI: Baker Book House, 1988).

Eusebius. *The Church History*. Translated by Paul L. Maier. Grand Rapids, MI: Kregel Publications, 1999.

Eusebius. *Church History.* Translated by Arthur Cushman McGiffert. In *Nicene and Post-Nicene Fathers*, 2nd series, vol. 1. Edited by Philip Schaff and Henry Wace. Buffalo, NY: Christian Literature Publishing Co., 1890. https://www.newadvent.org/fathers/250108.htm.

Evans, C. Stephen. *Pocket Dictionary of Apologetics & Philosophy of Religion*. Downers Grove, IL: InterVarsity Press, 2002.

Exell, Joseph S. *The Biblical Illustrator: Matthew* (Grand Rapids, MI: Baker Book House, 1952).

Ferguson, Everett. *Church History, Volume One: From Christ to the Pre-Reformation: The Rise and Growth of the Church in Its Cultural, Intellectual, and Political Context*. 2nd ed. Grand Rapids, MI: Zondervan, 2013.

Davie, Martin, Tim Grass, Stephen R. Holmes, John McDowell, and T. A. Noble, eds. *New Dictionary of Theology: Historical and Systematic*. London; Downers Grove, IL: Inter-Varsity Press; Inter-Varsity Press, 2016.

Dutt, Manmatha Nath, trans. *A Prose English Translation of Harivaṃśa*. Calcutta: H. C. Dass, 1897. Accessed November 12, 2025. https://www.gutenberg.org/cache/epub/61937/pg61937-images.html#chapter-lix-birth-of-krishna-and-baladeva.

Foreman, Benjamin A. "Matthew's Birth Narrative," in *Lexham Geographic Commentary on the Gospels*, ed. Barry J. Beitzel and Kristopher A. Lyle, Lexham Geographic Commentary (Bellingham, WA: Lexham Press, 2016).

González, Justo L., ed. *The Westminster Dictionary of Theologians*. Louisville, KY; London: Westminster John Knox Press, 2006.

Gilmore, Alec. "Tertullian," in *A Concise Dictionary of Bible Origins and Interpretation* (London; New York: T&T Clark, 2006).

Gregory of Nazianzus. *Oration 38: On the Theophany, or On the Nativity of Christ.* In *Nicene and Post-Nicene Fathers*, Second Series, Vol. 7. Edited by Philip Schaff and Henry Wace. New York: Christian Literature Publishing Co., 1894. Accessed November 3, 2025. https://www.newadvent.org/fathers/310238.htm.

Grisson, Fred A. in *Holman Illustrated Bible Dictionary*, ed. Chad Brand et al. (Nashville, TN: Holman Bible Publishers, 2003).

Handy, Lowell K. "Tammuz (Deity)." In *The Anchor Yale Bible Dictionary*, edited by David Noel Freedman. New York: Doubleday, 1992.

Hartranft, Chester D. "Augustine: Anti-Donatist Writings: Introductory Essay," in *St. Augustin: The Writings against the Manichaeans and against the Donatists*, ed. Philip Schaff, vol. 4, A Select Library of the Nicene and Post-Nicene Fathers of the Christian Church, First Series (Buffalo, NY: Christian Literature Company, 1887).

Haykin, Michael A. G., ed. *The Essential Lexham Dictionary of Church History*. Bellingham, WA: Lexham Press, 2022.

Hijmans, Steven E. *Sol: Image and Meaning of the Sun in Roman Art and Religion, Volume I*. Leiden, Netherlands: Brill, 2024.

Hippolytus of Rome. *Chronicon*. Translated by T. C. Schmidt in *Calculating December 25 as the Birth of Jesus*. 2010. https://tcschmidt.com/publications.

Hippolytus of Rome. *Commentary on Daniel*. Translated by T. C. Schmidt. 2010. Available at https://tcschmidt.com/publications

Hislop, Alexander. *The Two Babylons*. Annotated edition. Kindle edition.

Hislop, Alexander. *The Two Babylons: Or the Papal Worship Proved to Be the Worship of Nimrod and His Wife*. London: S. W. Partridge & Co., 1858. PDF.

Historia Augusta. "The Life of Saturninus." In Scriptores Historiae Augustae, translated by David Magie. Vol. 3. Loeb Classical Library 263. Cambridge, MA: Harvard University Press, 1932.

Holding, James Patrick. *Shattering the Christ Myth*. Xulon Press, 2008.

Huey, F. B. *Jeremiah, Lamentations*. Vol. 16. The New American Commentary. Nashville: Broadman & Holman Publishers, 1993.

Irenaeus. *Against Heresies*. In *The Ante-Nicene Fathers*, Vol. 1, edited by Alexander Roberts and James Donaldson. Buffalo, NY: Christian Literature Publishing Co., 1885.

Irving, Washington. *A History of New York*. By Diedrich Knickerbocker. New York: Inskeep & Bradford, 1809.

Keener, Craig S., *The IVP Bible Background Commentary: New Testament* (Downers Grove, IL: InterVarsity Press, 1993).

Keener, Craig S. *Matthew*, vol. 1, The IVP New Testament Commentary Series (Downers Grove, IL: InterVarsity Press, 1997).

Krause, Mark. "Wise Men, Magi," in *The Lexham Bible Dictionary*, ed. John D. Barry et al. (Bellingham, WA: Lexham Press, 2016).

Jackson, Samuel Macauley, ed. *The New Schaff-Herzog Encyclopedia of Religious Knowledge*. New York; London: Funk & Wagnalls, 1908–1914.

Jones, Timothy Paul. *Christian History Made Easy*. Torrance, CA: Rose Publishing, 2017.

Josephus. *The Antiquities of the Jews*. Translated by G. A. Williamson. Revised by E. Mary Smallwood. New York: Penguin Books, 1981.

Josephus. *The Jewish War*. Translated by G. A. Williamson. Revised by E. Mary Smallwood. New York: Penguin Books, 1981.

Larsen, Timothy, ed. *The Oxford Handbook of Christmas*. London, England: Oxford University Press, 2020.

Lendering, Jona. "Semiramis." *Livius.org*. Accessed November 15, 2025. https://www.livius.org/articles/mythology/semiramis/.

Lesko, Barbara S. *The Great Goddesses of Egypt the Great Goddesses of Egypt*. Norman, OK: University of Oklahoma Press, 2021.

Liefeld, Walter L. "Luke." In *The Expositor's Bible Commentary: Matthew, Mark, Luke*, edited by Frank E. Gaebelein, Vol. 8. Grand Rapids, MI: Zondervan Publishing House, 1984.

Macrobius. *The Saturnalia*. Translated with an introduction and notes by Percival Vaughan Davies. New York: Columbia University Press, 1969.

Magnússon, Eiríkr, Jessie L. Weston, William Morris, and Rasmus B. Anderson. *The Völsunga Saga*. London & New York: Norrœna Society, 1907. Accessed November 16, 2025. https://archive.org/details/volsungasaga00eir

Mansfield, Rick. "Best Septuagint (LXX) Translations." *Logos* (blog). September 2, 2025. https://www.logos.com/grow/best-septuagint-lxx-translations/#:~:text=The%20origins%20and%20name%20of,sincerely%20believed%20in%20ancient%20times

Martens, Elmer A. "Jeremiah." In *Evangelical Commentary on the Bible*, Vol. 3, Baker Reference Library, 529. Grand Rapids, MI: Baker Book House, 1995.

Matthews, Victor Harold, Mark W. Chavalas, and John H. Walton. *The IVP Bible Background Commentary: Old Testament*. Electronic ed. Downers Grove, IL: InterVarsity Press, 2000.

M'Clintock, John, and James Strong. "Nicholas (St.) of Myra." In *Cyclopædia of Biblical, Theological, and Ecclesiastical Literature*, VII:60–62. New York: Harper & Brothers, Publishers, 1894.

M'Clintock, John. and Strong, James. "Tertullian(us), Quintus Septimius Florens," in *Cyclopædia of Biblical, Theological, and Ecclesiastical Literature* (New York: Harper & Brothers, Publishers, 1881).

McClintock, John, and James Strong. "Yule." In *Cyclopædia of Biblical, Theological, and Ecclesiastical Literature*, Supplement—A–Z, 1012. New York: Harper & Brothers, Publishers, 1894.

McConville, J. Gordon. "Jeremiah." In *New Bible Commentary: 21st Century Edition*, edited by D. A. Carson et al., 4th ed., 682. Leicester, England; Downers Grove, IL: Inter-Varsity Press, 1994.

McDaniel, Spencer. "No, Santa Is Not Inspired by Odin." *Tales of Times Forgotten*. December 27, 2021. https://talesoftimesforgotten.com/2021/12/27/no-santa-claus-is-not-inspired-by-odin/.

McDaniel, Spencer. "The Long, Strange, Fascinating History of Santa Claus." *Tales of Times Forgotten*. December 7, 2019. https://talesoftimesforgotten.com/2019/12/07/the-long-strange-fascinating-history-of-santa-claus/.

McGowan, Andrew. "How December 25 Became Christmas." *Bible History Daily*. Biblical Archaeology Society, December 3, 2017. https://www.biblicalarchaeology.org/daily/people-cultures-in-the-bible/jesus-historical-jesus/how-december-25-became-christmas/

Moore, Clement Clarke. "A Visit from St. Nicholas." *Troy Sentinel*, December 23, 1823.

Musurillo, Herbert Anthony. *The Acts of the Christian Martyrs*. London, England: Oxford University Press, 1972.

Nast, Thomas. "Santa Claus in Camp." *Harper's Weekly*, January 3, 1863.

Nichols, Christopher. "From Jól to Yule." *Scandinavian Archaeology*. December 23, 2021. https://www.scandinavianarchaeology.com/from-jol-to-yule/.

Norden, Eduard. *Die Geburt des Kindes* [*The Birth of the Child*] (Leipzig: Teubner, 1924).

Porter, H. "Tammuz." In *The International Standard Bible Encyclopaedia*, edited by James Orr, John L. Nuelsen, Edgar Y. Mullins, and Morris O. Evans. Vol. 1–5. Chicago: The Howard-Severance Company, 1915.

Plutarch. *Moralia* Vol. V: *On Isis and Osiris*. Accessed November 12, 2025. https://penelope.uchicago.edu/Thayer/E/Roman/Texts/Plutarch/Moralia/Isis_and_Osiris*/D.html#T377b.

Roll, Susan. *Toward the Origins of Christmas*. Grand Rapids, MI: William B Eerdmans Publishing, 1996.

Schachterle, Joshua. "Did St. Nicholas Actually Attend the Council of Nicaea?" *Bart D. Ehrman Blog*. December 12, 2023. https://www.bartehrman.com/did-st-nicholas-actually-attend-the-council-of-nicaea/.

Schaff, Philip, and Henry Wace, eds. *Eusebius: Church History, Life of Constantine the Great, and Oration in Praise of Constantine*. Vol. 1. A Select Library of the Nicene and Post-Nicene Fathers of the Christian Church, Second Series. New York: Christian Literature Company, 1890.

Schmidt, T. C. *Calculating December 25 as the Birth of Jesus*. 2010. https://tcschmidt.com/publications.

Simpson, Jacqueline, and Steve Roud. *A Dictionary of English Folklore*. London, England: Oxford University Press, 2017.

St. Nicholas Center. "Bishop Nicholas Loses His Cool." Accessed November 16, 2024. https://www.stnicholascenter.org/who-is-st-nicholas/stories-legends/traditional-stories/life-of-nicholas/bishop-nicholas-loses-his-cool

Sturluson, Snorri. *Heimskringla: The Chronicle of the Kings of Norway*. Translated by Samuel Laing. Revised with notes by Rasmus B. Anderson. Vol. 1. London: Norrœna Society, 1907.

Talley, Thomas J. *The Origins of the Liturgical Year: Second, Emended Edition*. New York, NY: Pueblo Publishing, 1991.

Taylor, Robert. *The Diegesis: Being a Discovery of the Origin, Evidences, and Early History of Christianity* (London: R. Carlile, 1829)

Tertullian. *Adversus Judaeos* [*Against the Jews*]. In *Ante-Nicene Fathers*, Vol. 3. Edited by Alexander Roberts and James Donaldson. Buffalo, NY: Christian Literature Publishing Co., 1885.

Tertullian. *The Apology of Tertullian.* Translated by S. Thelwall. London: Society for Promoting Christian Knowledge, 1908. https://dn790000.ca.archive.org/0/items/apologyoftertull00tert/apologyoftertull00tert.pdf

Tertullian. *On Idolatry*. Chap. 15. In *The Ante-Nicene Fathers*, Vol. 3, edited by Alexander Roberts and James Donaldson. Buffalo, NY: Christian Literature Publishing Co., 1885. Accessed November 16, 2025. https://www.newadvent.org/fathers/0302.htm.

Thompson, Stephen E. *Ancient Egypt: Facts and Fictions*. Santa Barbara, CA: ABC-CLIO, 2019.

Trites, Allison A., Larker, William J., *Cornerstone Biblical Commentary, Vol 12: The Gospel of Luke and Acts* (Carol Stream, IL: Tyndale House Publishers, 2006).

Turner, David and Bock, Darrell L. *Cornerstone Biblical Commentary, Vol 11: Matthew and Mark* (Carol Stream, IL: Tyndale House Publishers, 2005).

Wells, Sara. "Tammuz." In *The Lexham Bible Dictionary*, edited by John D. Barry, David Bomar, Derek R. Brown, Rachel Klippenstein, Douglas Mangum, Carrie Sinclair Wolcott, Lazarus Wentz,

Elliot Ritzema, and Wendy Widder. Bellingham, WA: Lexham Press, 2016.

Wheeler, Frank E. "Dionysius (Person)." In *The Anchor Yale Bible Dictionary*, edited by David Noel Freedman. New York: Doubleday, 1992.

Williams, Frank. *The Panarion of Epiphanius of Salamis: Books II and III*. Leiden: Brill, 1994.

Woodrow, Ralph. "The Two Babylons: A Case Study in Poor Methodology." *Christian Research Journal*, Apr. 9, 2009. CRI / Equip.org website. https://www.equip.org/articles/the-two-babylons/.

Van Dyke, Henry. "The Oak of Geismar." *Scribner's Magazine* 10 (July–December 1891): 681–87.

VectorMine. "Earth's Seasons Diagram." *iStockphoto* Stock Illustration ID: 942149808. Licensed for use by the author.

Zhang, Meiqiao. 2023. "Whence the 8th Day of the 4th Lunar Month as the Buddha's Birthday" *Religions* 14, no. 4: 451. https://doi.org/10.3390/rel14040451

About the Author

Elder Kevin L. Betton, Jr. is an Army Chaplain, educator, and apologist committed to equipping believers with a deeper understanding of Scripture. Born in Niagara Falls, NY, he has served in the United States Army since 2002—first as a Religious Affairs Specialist and later as a Chaplain, commissioned in 2019 and promoted to Captain in 2021. He holds a Bachelor of Science in Religion (*Magna Cum Laude*) and a Master of Divinity with distinction, both from Liberty University, and is currently pursuing a Doctor of Philosophy in Bible Exposition.

A licensed minister since 2004 and ordained Elder since 2007, Elder Betton has dedicated more than two decades to preaching, teaching, and discipleship. He is the founder of the Greater Works Discipleship Academy, an online platform providing seminary-level education for pastors, leaders, and believers worldwide. His digital resources—used across churches and ministries—address topics such as apologetics, biblical studies, and the intersection of faith and culture.

He and his wife, Celeste, reside in Texas with their three children: Kyndal, Mikayla, and Judah.

www.ingramcontent.com/pod-product-compliance
Lightning Source LLC
LaVergne TN
LVHW091543070526
838199LV00002B/185